'Celtic Christianity [barcode: C000276816] would an urban co[...] in their worship? S[...] book jewels from be[...] from a very different era that struck them with a sense of joy and wonder. He was to find that in his own congregation the style of worship, echoing ancient rhythms that embrace poetry and the imagination, still has the power to fire our faith and help his flock to grow. His book pulls back the curtain of modernity and explores what it is that chimes with our inner being. For lovers of Celtic Christianity there is much here to inspire, but for the sceptics he also skilfully examined the concerns, and in so doing, he presents a case that will encourage every congregation to embrace this ancient expression of the faith.'

Colin Blakely, Editor,
Church of England Newspaper

'I would like to warmly commend *The Divine Spark*. Steve's writing is warm and engaging and gives us a valuable insight into Celtic Christianity. A spirituality that has much to teach the church about creation "that bears God's footprint", the desire to grow community in a world that idolises individualism and consumerism, as well as encouraging us to have eyes and hearts open to glimmers of glory all around us.

Steve not only writes with great enthusiasm on Celtic Christianity but is someone who tries his very best to live it! A timely book and very much worth a read.'

Revd Canon Phil Stone, Community Leader and Director of the Scargill Movement

'Steve has found a spirituality that resonates with today's big questions, needs and longings and has woven the two together in his book. He writes as someone eager to share his own renewal of a sense of wonder and friendship with the same Lord who was known and experienced by our Celtic ancestors in the faith.'

Revd Dr Liz Hoare, Wycliffe Hall, Oxford

'This is translucent writing with touches of poetry; it catches the light with its honesty and insights. The writer is a beachcomber of life sharing his tenderest treasures. I found it page-turning, accessible and profound.'

Isobel Thrilling, poet

The Divine Spark

Why Celtic wisdom can
refresh the church today

Foreword by Michael Mitton

STEVE MORRIS

Authentic

First published 2020 by Authentic Media Limited,
PO Box 6326, Bletchley, Milton Keynes, MK1 9GG.
authenticmedia.co.uk

British Library Cataloguing in Publication Data
A catalogue record for this book is available from the
British Library.
ISBN: 978-1-78893-177-9
978-1-78893-178-6 (e-book)

Cover design by Luke Porter
Printed and bound by CPI Group (UK) Ltd, Croydon, CR0 4YY

For Christine, fellow traveller

There is a door to which thou hast the key
Sole keeper thou.
There is a latch no hand can lift save thine.
Not crownèd brow,
Nor warrior, thinker, poet famed in time,
But only thou.
O heart make haste and bid Him to thy hearth;
Nay, urge Him in.[1]

Contents

CONTENTS

Foreword

In the early 1990s, those interested in Celtic Christian spirituality were mostly in the liberal and catholic traditions of the church. Those in the evangelical and charismatic streams of the church generally assumed that the Celtic way strayed dangerously close to the veneration of the saints, and that they had an interest in nature that sounded far too much like the language of the tree-hugging New-Agers. All that changed dramatically during the 90s, and many evangelicals and charismatics found a quarry of precious stones in the Christian history of Britain and Ireland that inspired new visions for how we serve Christ in this post-modern, post-Christendom era in which we now find ourselves.

Some wondered whether this would be a passing fad that would flare up in the life of the church and then die down when a new fashion replaced it. However, here we are, not far off thirty years of the revival of interest in Celtic Christianity, and we find that the fascination with the lives of the early Celtic missionaries and their witness to Christ is as alive as ever. Christians from a wide range of traditions continue to find inspiration in the early stories of the Celtic church in the lands of Britain and Ireland, and value the spirituality that is associated with it.

Steven writes as one such enthusiast who has done his own careful research into this spirituality. But he writes not just as an enthusiast, but as a thoughtful practitioner. He has identified insights, values and resources in Celtic Christianity, that he carefully applies not only to his own life and witness, but also to the way he is developing the ministry and mission of the North London church that he leads. Steven shares something of the story of how he has applied this spirituality in the life of his church, and so this is a very useful and practical book for any who have a love for Celtic Christianity and who also have any kind of leadership responsibility in their church.

Few would claim that Celtic Christianity is the answer to all the church's problems. But Steven's book is a helpful reminder that the vibrant spirituality that prevailed in the remarkable eruption of gospel life in the lands of Ireland and Britain from the fourth century onwards has much to say to us in our twenty-first century church. And who among the followers of Christ today don't long to see the re-emergence of joyful, dynamic communities of love and faith that not only provide a hospitable space for all enquirers, and also beautifully transform the communities where they live? Anything that helps towards that end is hugely valuable.

Michael Mitton
Canon Emeritus, Derby Cathedral

1

Edinburgh Thoughts

I love the Edinburgh Fringe. I go most summers. The city is full of people off to see different shows and different genres. In fact, it is so packed that often you get stuck in a huge queue of people on the way somewhere. It is a place where artists reign, where the creative imagination is in the driving seat.

As such, it offers an interesting way of seeing the world upside-down. The normal rules don't apply. This is what it would be like if artists ruled the world.

One evening, on the way back from a show, a nice young person handed me a little card that said 'Jesus loves you, come and find out more'. I followed an arrow and found myself in a room up two flights of stairs, in a building down a side street.

There was a worship band playing classic evangelical songs and about 15 folk watching. It may, of course, have filled up and swelled with people later on, but it seemed to me that this was an *alternative* to the Fringe – with all its ribaldry, irreverence and drinking. It was a way of perhaps bringing Jesus into the Fringe. But I felt forlorn and wondered why this was so. The thought was gnawing away at me that Jesus was *already* at the Fringe, but it was hard to put my finger on why I felt a bit desolate. Perhaps it was because I couldn't but notice that there were so many thousands of people apparently able to ignore the lure of finding out more about Jesus.

I wonder what our Celtic forebears would have made of this evangelism tactic? If they could beam up or down 1,500 years what would they do? How would *they* be in contact with the world around them?

Of course, before we go much further, we need to be clear about our terms. Celtic Christianity really refers to ways of thinking of and doing Christianity and church that were common in the Celtic-speaking world of the early Middle Ages. The whole area is not without controversy and I hope not to get too deep into this. Perhaps, what we can say at the moment is that Celtic Christianity is about some of the traditions of the British and Irish and ways of doing church and faith that were very distinctive. As we continue, the differences and distinctiveness will make themselves known – but we need always to have the humility to know that, at this distance, much of what we suppose is conjecture.

Ian Bradley, in his wonderful book *The Celtic Way*,[1] points out that the Celtic Christians had a particular theology that emphasised that all people had the divine spark within them. They wanted to liberate that spark in people rather than impose a new creed on them.

For them, the pagan religion was not a threat that had to be got rid of – it was not a heresy. Instead, it was itself a stirring, a wanting, a yearning even. It was a reaching out to God. Rather than tear down the existing standing stones and the like, the Celtic Christians looked to 'baptise' them, to incorporate them into Christian worship. They walked alongside their fellow spiritual travellers and looked for what was good about what was already happening.

This, of course, was quite the opposite of the other Christian presence I encountered in Edinburgh – a fellow on the Royal Mile bellowing out propositional truth about our dear Lord. He was there every day, on a footstall next to a big white cross, plastered with Bible verses. He's there every year and each year I find it sad. Perhaps the only time fringe-goers get to even think about God involves feeling anger and dismay at religion delivered through a megaphone. I am sure that he does more harm than good.

Could the ancients have a little clue for us moderns about how to help people to want to 'come and see'?

I wonder if our Celtic forebears *had* managed to time-travel to Edinburgh whether, rather than trying to bend the reality that people were experiencing they would be blessing what was good in it and walking alongside them – fellow humans in the image of a good God? They might have celebrated the glorious creativity of the event and seen God in it or applauded the bold questioning of a society where social justice is needed more than ever. They might have sung and danced with musicians. They might have stopped to pat one of the lovely dogs walking by and revel in the glory of creation and the gift to us of our animal friends. They might have had a glass or two of wonderful Scotch and enjoyed for a moment the chance to sit and sup and be with friends old and new.

And had they done this, perhaps the people might have wondered why these folk seemed so peaceful and full of joy. They might have marvelled in their tales of adventure and pilgrimage and wondered whether they were called to a fresh start as well. It is no accident that Celtic missionaries and saints by and large avoided getting killed by those to whom they took the good news. They knew the terrors of evil and they knew the fragility of life, but they began from a theology that stressed the essential goodness of creation and were optimistic about human nature, the power of hospitality and friendship.

The Fringe is well-named. It began as a festival for those acts that couldn't get a look-in at the official show. The Celtic Christians were also fringe people who didn't fit in with the mainstream (although for a few centuries they defined the Christian faith in some of the old outposts of the Roman Empire). These days, Celtic Christianity again feels very on the fringe. But this ancient tradition and spirituality can help the modern Church – not by replacing what we have, but by helping us to think about some things anew and to deepen our spiritual connection with God.

But perhaps it isn't only the Celtic spirituality that is on the fringe. We certainly live in a post-Christian age. The faith has been, and will continue to be, pushed to the margins. We need to learn to live more from the edge of things. We are not first port of call, although we are still a voice calling into the lives of others. But perhaps we can learn from our forebears who themselves were at the margins and were able to have a huge impact on culture from the fringe of these islands. Speaking from the margins is an opportunity to do differently.

How would it be if we 'baptised' the much that is good about modern life? If we showed just how much we understood the sense of seeking that is behind so much of what our society thinks about and does, then we might find a new connection with people.

I write this book as an evangelical, a leader of a Church of England charismatic/evangelical church in London. I love being an evangelical and I am very optimistic about both the church and the spiritual space that I and so many others inhabit. I hope that this book celebrates all that is good about Church, and if I fail in this at any point I apologise and put it down to overenthusiasm. I have sometimes commented on blind-spots in my own spiritual tradition, but only gently and only as a reminder to myself, mainly, to think again every so often.

This is no academic treatise. There are some excellent and detailed books out there on Celtic

Christianity. I am not a lifelong follower of the Celtic way. But I have become interested in how connecting with Celtic Christianity can play a part in growing a church like ours and revitalising some areas of our ministry and worship. I have done it not to throw out what is strong about our spirituality. Instead, I want to add to what we already have.

I have also become fascinated by the way that some of the beautiful poems and prayers of the Celtic Christians, collected more than a century ago by a small group of amateur ethnographers, have a way of speaking very strongly to modern Christians and other seekers on the pilgrim way.

> I came to the Cross, the dew still wet upon it, and knelt down. I cried 'O my dear Lord, wilt Thou not spell me the secret of Thy Passion, or thy brave out-during of death and pain?' At which he whispered gently, 'Beloved go and live thy life in the spirit of My dying, in righteousness and love, then truly shalt thou share My victory and taste my peace.'[2]

This kind of illuminated jewel of a poem-prayer has the ability to jerk us awake in our spiritual search. The use of the personal pronoun allows us to inhabit it. We find the Cross covered in dew – perhaps the tears of nature herself. At the Cross is a pilgrim who has come there, by we know not which way. Like many of us they may have stumbled upon this site of terror and redemption almost by accident.

We kneel with the poet and are fellow pilgrims, asking the great question that so many of us have. We suddenly think anew of the suffering of Christ and his bravery. And in that moment the Christ tenderly whispers to us his counsel and words of hope. The Celtic poetry and prayers speak loudly to us because they are spoken softly with a different timbre to much that we hear in the world. In a noisy room the quiet voice sometimes stands out. That's one of those paradoxes.

This is a poem that is rooted and earthy and offers a sharp and perhaps fresh picture of Christ and the way he speaks to us. It reassures us that we are beloved of the King of Kings, and in a regular church context, it can create a sense of awe in its beauty and rustic finesse.

It also helps us to see Jesus in our context, our locale. We begin to experience a localised Jesus – a good counterbalance to the Lord who bestrides the universe.

This will not replace what we have, but as an offering to the modern church it is invaluable, and many folk have no idea that these riches still exist. And the sense of the sheer and abiding closeness of God is a real tonic to us weary disciples, worn down by mass capitalism and consumerism and terrified by the horrors of pandemics and all that goes with them.

2

In the Beginning . . .

Early days

As a boy I would read J. R. R. Tolkien's *The Lord of the Rings* over and over again. Every summer holiday I would break up from school and breathe again – ready to start the great quest with Gandalf, Frodo Baggins and the gang. This magical experience was repeated each year until well into my teens. And as I got older the film version by Peter Jackson relit the fires of interest and awe.

I loved to be in the world of Middle Earth. I was immersed in its deeper magic. It wasn't just the story that so grabbed me. It was the sense of the creation of an entire world – one in which nature loomed large, wonder was always present and the big struggle between good and evil was a reality. Like many others, I had the vague suspicion that in olden times the wonderful seemed to be closer and more accessible.

The odd thing was that the world of Middle Earth seemed way more immediate and real to me than much of the world I encountered day to day. This wasn't simple escapism. My journey with Tolkien had an impact on my life and, although I didn't realise it at the time, it was the wonder that I encountered in my boyhood reading that opened me up for my own conversion in my forties. Oddly, I had no problem believing the epic-narrative of God because I had lived a little in this kind of world as a boy.

After a while, what surprised me was that the sense of joy and transcendence and the wonder of the world wasn't really happening in my faith. I was seeking for joy. I think I was trying too hard and then judging myself that the holy thing wasn't happening. It was only a short jump from there to feeling bad about myself. On such psychological loops rest a lot of unhappiness.

I am sure I am not alone in experiencing a sense of joy and wonder and wanting more of it. C. S. Lewis talks most movingly about his own encounter with ineffable joy and his slow move towards the God who is beyond the simple materialist world.

Perhaps, as for many modern people, this prescient un-modernity was never totally extinguished in me. Indeed, the sense of yearning for this kind of connectivity and sense of 'magic' is shared by many others. The world is full of wonder. We all feel that there is more to life than we can touch.

On a chill winter night looking up at the moon and stars we feel the immensity of creation and know that there is something amazing about our home planet. Things feel connected. We get a sense of how life is a gift and we wonder who that gift came from and who we should live it for.

This sense is one of the reasons why we would do well not to write off our forebears in the faith, who felt very close to the wonders of the natural world. As a church leader I have learned that a connection with Celtic spirituality can help a congregation grow – in numbers and faith, and that the lessons of the ancient faith speak deeply into a modern world that our Celtic forebears could hardly have imagined. If they could time-travel to our world, how might they look upon skyscrapers and cars and aeroplanes? The things we take for granted would be pure wonder to them.

Beware romanticising

Much has been written about Celtic Christianity and much of it is very good and thought-provoking. Some voices on the edge of the debate have prompted us not to romanticise the past. They point out that, although we might paint the Celtic Christians as free spirits and so claim them as an antidote to modern managerialism, they too had management structures and bishops. Others point out that the actual primary material from the period is woefully thin and that it's hard to claim a distinctive Celtic anything.

Still others point out that the ethnographic poems and prayers collected more than 100 years ago were edited by the listeners and so may not be as authentic as we first thought.

But even if the history is a little slippery it may not matter all that much. We may be projecting on to the Celtic idea precisely because of a deep yearning for a different kind of church from the one we have. And we need to listen to what this yearning has to tell us.

Whatever the case, we need to temper our enthusiasm with a dose of scepticism. Peter Ryder's funny song *Holy Columba* allows us to poke a little gentle fun at the Celtic 'industry'.

> It's all so romantic, it's driving us frantic
> A publishing boom, and our sites are all set
> as Northumbrian clergy put out new liturgy
> with interlace borders, on the internet.[1]

It seems to me that anyone who writes about Celtic spirituality is stepping into a world that at least has some politics about it. Maybe a better way is to say it has history and a great desire to protect the traditions and truths of this precious spirituality. But I *have* stepped into the breach and this book aims to answer questions that have been burning in my mind for a long time. They mainly derive from my own journey as an evangelical and church minister. These are just a few of my questions:

1. Can we get an even greater sense of wonder about the world we live in? Is there a place for a renewed sense of creation and God's hand in it? Can this be, should this be, more central to what we hear in church and the way we do community together?

2. Where is God in our workplaces and homes? How close is he and can we reclaim these places as centres of holiness?

3. How do we incorporate imagination, poetry and creativity into our worship and prayer? Can we become a new generation of poets and writers – inspired by the author of life?

4. Can we be the place seekers come to for discussion about the things they care about? What do we say to those who feel our planet is threatened, who are dismayed by war, who despair at patriarchal supremacy, who know that there is something special in the arts and music, who wonder why the church can sometimes seem stuck on other issues that appear trivial? Is it only the comedians who can provoke us to think? What does the church have to say about the evils of structural racism?

5. What does leading the good life look like, and how can we feel more balanced between work, worship and family?

There are many other questions. But I know that when I began reading about and tuning into Celtic poetry, prayers and stories and the lives of the saints, I began to breathe more lightly in my faith. It was a huge relief. It felt as if I had access to a new spiritual lung.

I would like to understand why, and whether the answer to this can unlock new ways of doing evangelical (and any other) church, building on all that is good already.

Re-examining evangelical church – thinking about a new service

A good friend of mine once commented that the problem with church is that it seems too 'human-focused'. I think I know what he meant. Amid the clamour of a service is there room for something older, simpler and quieter? We want to somehow enlarge the envelope of God's goodness – to get a sense of his love for the creatures we share our planet with. Someone once told me that they loved Celtic spirituality because it was 'earthy'. Others have commented that the Celtic way seems gentler and kinder than the version of the faith they have sometimes been served up. It seems to meet a need.

Research suggests that others are looking for something away from what is ordinarily on offer – that they see something authentic in a more ancient way of worshipping God. Evensong at Westminster Abbey saw a 30% increase in attendance between 2008 and 2012.[2] Millennials say they wish they could find a way of slowing down.[3] Add to this that only 0.5% of 18–24-year-olds attend an Anglican church service at all[4] and it looks as though there might be some room for rediscovering a tradition that is older and allows time to think and be silent. The old as well as the new has something to offer.

On a practical level, I was wondering what on earth to do with an evening service that was struggling to attract people. None of us wanted to close it down, but we needed a new focus for it, a new energy.

I don't think I am alone in enjoying a Sunday evening service. I enjoy a Sunday evening service for reasons that stretch right back into my childhood. Even as a small child I always seemed to get a bit nervous and restless as Sunday progressed. That still happens to me today. It is perhaps a throw-back to dreading going to school on a Monday. By Sunday evening I need something to reassure me that things are going to be OK and the week ahead is nothing to be feared.

So what about the evening service? I started researching the life of our saint, St Cuthbert. And I visited the place where he lived and worked – Lindisfarne. I took a pilgrimage – something I talk about later as one of the great gifts of the Celtic tradition. One day while listening to the seals and their calls to each other, I remember being so struck by how peaceful God is and how this peace was a gift for me and for all. In this 'thin place' it was possible to gain more of a perspective.

I began reading and enjoying Celtic liturgies and poems and began sharing these with my congregation. It surprised me how much they enjoyed these pieces of writing and how they always asked me for more.

And so we decided to launch a Sunday evening Celtic service. We are just regular churchgoers in a suburban evangelical church with charismatic leanings, with an ear for words and a sense that there was room to add a string to our spiritual bow. We remain evangelical and charismatic but we saw something in the Celtic tradition that both chimed with what we already had and added something we were missing.

And so we began a Sunday evening Celtic service. We expected a handful, but from the start it became our second-best attended service of the month. There is something about the old religion, the 'deeper magic' as C. S. Lewis put it, that chimed with us, and our feeling is that it would chime in many other evangelical and charismatic churches. We have come to realise that many people feel anxious and alone and oddly oppressed on a Sunday evening. They face the week ahead. They worry about their jobs and a bullying boss, or fear for their children or relatives.

They respond to a Sunday Celtic service because it seems to offer deep comfort and reassurance. In the service's ancient rhythms, care of nature, talk of saints and angels and a chance just to *be* is like having a warm cocoa before going to bed. That can be no bad thing. But more than that, it meets a massive unmet need – the need to feel protected.

Choosing to do a Celtic service isn't to ditch everything else, get your skates on and head up to Iona. You can add a service that is Celtic as a way of scratching a spiritual itch while still staying true to the majority-spirituality in your church – be that evangelical or charismatic.

This may seem like spiritual consumerism or raiding the treasures of others. Our approach certainly has some degree of pragmatism – but now we are here on the Celtic road we have no intention of turning back, individually or as a church.

This book is unashamedly about the impact of the Celtic tradition on our congregation and it is a recommendation to all churches to look again at what this spirituality has to offer. I hope that it is written with reverence and love and a sense of boyish wonder that our God is glorious and that we have much to learn from the past.

Dark forces and what to do about them

I came to faith in a Pentecostal church that had a strong sense of supernatural forces and spiritual warfare. I retain that insight. The world often seems like a dark and dangerous place with forces acting beyond our control.

This was one of the first and most important con-nections I found with the Celtic tradition. They *also* understood their physical vulnerability too – illness, disease and lawlessness were constant threats. It was hard to feel safe, even within a village sur-rounded by friends and family. What do we do when it can all be snatched away in an instant?

Our Celtic forebears had a strong sense of spiritual attack and their poems and liturgies speak directly into this battle. St Cuthbert, our saint at my church, fought a lifelong battle with the devil – who was as real to him as his brother monks. The terrors of de-mons and dark forces haunted his steps and he did battle with the thoughts and feelings these engen-dered till his dying day on a windswept island.

Interestingly, many unchurched people have a strong sense of spiritual peril too. Just spend a few hours talking about this to them and you'll hear stories that would have sounded very familiar to the Celts.

The Celtic tradition speaks into this other-worldliness and is very strong indeed to modern ears. Spiritual warfare is a central part of the Celtic tradition. This speaks loudly to us today – even in our technological age. The old demons and darkness cannot be swept away quite so easily as we think. The world is ancient and ancient forces have not packed their bags and gone home. Much of our modern security is a thin veneer. The darkness is still the darkness.

St Patrick stood strong at the druid stronghold at Tara. He kindled a fire in recognition of Christ's resurrection. He stood in the breach, aware of the powers of darkness and oppression. His mighty prayer calling on God's protection is as valid now as ever:

> This day I call to me . . . God's shield to protect me . . . from the snares of demons . . . from dark powers that assail me . . . for my shield this day I call a mighty power, the Holy Trinity.[5]

It also introduces us to the great power and beauty of the Celtic way with words. Without wishing to be rude about modern worship songs, many of which I love and build my faith, the sheer power and beauty of Patrick's well-chosen words and images perhaps explain why people today respond so powerfully to them.

The idea of calling on God's protection and of his mighty shield is potent. We need protection. After all, what is our obsession with insurance, other than an attempt to mitigate risk in a world that is full of uncertainty? The terrible sense of oppression we sometimes feel, knowing about the snares of the devil and demons, is palpable – my friend once described this as the feeling of being caught in a pair of pliers and squeezed.

The sense of being assailed is common in our high-pressure remorseless world. We sometimes can't put a word to it and we frequently medicalise it as stress or anxiety – which of course can be debilitating medical conditions.

But amongst our young people we hear reported an epidemic of anxiety – partly caused by social media and societal pressure. Celtic Christians understood the feeling of oppression and I have a sense that they would empathise with us and know where we were coming from. Their beautiful prayers do no harm and have a magnetism born of the reality they describe and the sense of hope they share in God's ability to surround and protect us when we have a failure of courage or morale, or an emotional wobble.

The magnificent invocation of the mighty power of the Trinity is more certain to invoke courage in us than many a stirring Sunday talk on the Trinity. The deep sense that the Trinity is a source of protection is a winning insight. The very image here helps to explain the Trinity in a way that is both reassuring and logical.

> In the Name of the Three,
> In the name of their might
> I will draw the ring
> That doth instant bring
> Safety from foes' affright.
> In the Name of the Three
> I shall rout all my fears,
> I shall stand all unscathed
> from the cast of their spears;
> Thus shall I know no overthrow.[6]

If we feel a need for a dose of poetry and the imagination that fires it up, this is a good place to start. With our Celtic forebears we can once again experience it and start to live our faith out in ways that nurture and encourage us. We can all benefit from drawing the ring of God's protection around our lives. Who isn't in need of routing their fears? Which of us could resist standing unscathed after one of the many battles of life?

3

The Right Time for the Celtic Tradition?

As I was starting on this book I told my daughter what I was intending to write. With the 'confidence' of a teenager, she said to me, 'Dad, why on earth would you want to write about all that weird stuff? – we don't need that tradition, we have one of our own. Isn't it all made up anyway?'

Now you may say this was a little harsh. But I think that my daughter's sentiment is actually shared by many others. The Celtic tradition, at least from the outside, can look a bit soft and fluffy. That can be countered, I think – although the adoption of elements of Celticism by New Age sources has led to some suspicions. Is it a short step from an interest in Celtic Christianity to wearing magical amulets and the like?

What is true is that the established Church has sometimes been hostile to Celtic culture and spirituality.

In the Western Isles of Scotland the established Church attempted to suppress the Celtic tradition – its prayers, music and customs. The harsh Calvinism of the Church of Scotland, with its obsession with sinfulness and the total fallenness of people, ran counter to the Celtic insistence on the essential goodness of God and his creation. Calvin and Augustine and their teachings were not easy to reconcile with the Celts.

One wonders if something of this still remains. While in Edinburgh I popped into the National Library to see if there were any books on Celtic Christianity. The very helpful librarian directed me to the correct place. They were filed under Mythology – which is a bit strange if you think about it, especially as we were no more than 200 paces from the church that St Columba founded. But, perhaps because the source material is scarce, that's what it seems like: a myth.

A constructed tradition

But as to whether it is all made up, that's another question. Ian Bradley's masterful book *Celtic Christianity: Making Myths and Chasing Dreams*[1] gives a very full explanation of where the Celtic ideas and 'tradition' came from. Bradley is nuanced about the idea of a golden age of Celtic Christianity. Where he is most interesting, at least for me, is in his highlighting that the Celtic material we have was almost wholly written after the age of the Celtic Christians. We lack manuscripts and archaeological evidence from the golden age itself – between the mid-fifth and mid-seventh centuries – although this lack of direct contemporary evidence for ancient history is not unusual.

So to some extent we do have a constructed reality and the power and romanticism of the Celtic idea have refused to die. This is not to say that we don't have sources – it is just that they have come along later, as often happens with other histories.

What we have is an ongoing process of rediscovery and reinvention. We have what we have.

We have a very unlikely hero to thank for some of the most powerful documents that we have about our Celtic forebears. He came along just in time, it seems. Alexander Carmichael was a civil servant in the Hebrides and West Coast of Scotland. As he got to speak and listen to local people he began to hear age-old poems, blessings and prayers from the centuries past. He collected this amazing oral history and wrote it down and the resulting *Carmina Gadelica*[2] speaks loudly of all that people love about Celtic spirituality – its earthiness, love of creation and the strong sense of a God who is very close. And there were others like Alistair Maclean who also collected ancient stories and praise. Like Carmichael, he did so with a glowing sense of wonder.

This little burst of activity has given us some valuable volumes of poems and prayers and incantations. The remembered words go back through the centuries and, even if they were edited, give us a strong sense of the poetry and place from which they came.

Now is the time

It has to be said that 'the right time' for Celtic spirituality has been declared just about every decade over the last 40 years. Indeed, there have been mini-revivals over the centuries. The inspired writing of David Adam,[3] one-time vicar of Lindisfarne, has kept the pot bubbling. Others have joined the fray. There is no shortage of resources.

There is now a small industry of books on Celtic spirituality. But is it fair to say that it remains a fringe interest? One wonders why the ancient 'Fire of the North' has not reignited. Why has it remained something of a secret, especially in mainstream churches? I have my theories, but I can't be sure. What I can say is that there have been ebbs and flows in the popularity of Celtic spirituality.

Perhaps the hold of the institutional Church has been so strong that it has stopped more experimental or unusual expressions of the faith coming through.

Perhaps the issue is critical mass. Ideas grow and become adopted when enough people hear about them and hear that they work. For there to be more Celtic services and a greater understanding of all that this spirituality offers it will take enough church leaders to see just what *is* on offer. That isn't as easy as it sounds. Celtic liturgy doesn't fit snugly or easily into existing patterns of liturgy.

And a Celtic service might sound counterintuitive to a church that sees creating worship bands, running Alpha courses and other thoroughly useful methods as the prime way of generating church growth. But our experience is that it isn't either/or and that the Celtic way adds something that we were lacking. It has helped us to reconsider creation, to create somewhere that is reflective and a way of looking at the world that, despite the centuries that have passed, is surprisingly modern.

To me it is one way and a very valuable one. As someone who loves poetry and words it is particularly appealing, but it may not be others' cup of tea.

One has the feeling that becoming a follower of the Celts is to need to be signed up to a slightly peculiar all-consuming society (like joining one of those battle-reenactment groups or taking part in a weekly folk evening). The growing of beards may be necessary. But perhaps that's just me.

My contention is that the time is right now for Celtic spirituality, and that it works well running alongside totally orthodox evangelical churches. It is a way of doing the faith that is ideally placed to add something new – or should that be old? Although it may be contentious, it seems to me that it isn't quite necessary to throw one's whole hat in with the Celts. But it is at least worth wondering what is on offer.

The Celtic way may never be mainstream and that is perhaps how it should be. But it could be much better known and it could help to inform the spirituality of a new generation of believers and seekers.

Why has the fire not ignited?

So how might we explain the strange case of Celtic spirituality – why has it remained on the margins, especially of evangelical church?

From the very earliest days there has been a fear that the Celtic way is simply poorly disguised pantheism. This is certainly a criticism worth entertaining and exploring. G. K. Chesterton pointed out the problem of regarding nature as Mother Nature.[4] His comment was that we should see nature as our sister – a prescient warning against the temptations of pantheism. The Celts, of course, celebrated the goodness of creation not only because of the beauty of the world around, but because God made it and Jesus is in charge of it.

Some fear that Celtic spiritualty may be New Age through the back door. Allied to this is the sense that just feeling wonder at God's creation doesn't really demand the sacrifice Jesus calls us to give. We may admire the world and all its creatures while never taking the decisive step towards Jesus. Others might say that the Celtic way is a bit soft on sin and repentance.

We might let these objections remain with us for a while – as we look later on at the Celtic sense of reverence and awe of nature and the God who makes it all possible. We can ask *then* if the charge of pantheism is proven and we can look at what the Celtic Christians really thought about sin and grace and original goodness. But what is for sure is that the Celtic Church was persecuted by the established Church.

I have heard others say that the Celtic way is a pastoral idyll with little to say to our modern and largely urban population. Perhaps it smacks of 'Merrie England' to some. One vicar said to me: 'I am an urban person; I don't feel any connection with all this nature stuff at all.'

A broader look at the spiritual map

So what is it like out there? What is the spiritual state of the nation? There are so many commentators that it really is a case of 'you pays your money and you takes your choice'. . . I want to add just snapshots. There are numerous ways of reading where we are now and this changes, it seems, almost monthly. One thing is for sure: the pandemic has changed everything and we can't be certain what our world and our communities will be like at the end of it. What is interesting is that the Celtic Way has so much to say to our current concerns and fears and uncertainties. The concentration on good communities, protection and creativity are all the more part of our spiritual search in these very hard times. It doesn't seem that this pandemic has extinguished religious faith – indeed, it has made some of us realise that we need God even more and that we are fragile creatures.

Of course, many of the things that were influencing the spiritual map before the pandemic are, and still will be, issues. Different political leaders change the temperature. Fears about youth culture, gang culture and a decline in numbers of churchgoers feed a sense of decline in the faith. How will a deadly virus play its part in the future?

Whatever we love about our consumerist world (and there is much to love) it certainly comes at a price. To some extent we are all infected with consumerism – it is the dominant 'religion' of the age. Consumerism has its temples and its priests and its rituals. We may not feel like victims but even the most hardened of shoppers may feel that you can't ever actually buy your way into happiness. But the impulse to buy and to own is very strong. Just perhaps, the glow of the old lamp might be enough to get us modern people to stop awhile and listen and wonder if there is more to life than acquiring. Many of us want to be made free from the desire to own everything we see and touch and just to enjoy being alive right here and right now.

Unchurched

For those who don't darken the doors of a church there is still a yearning for authenticity. The fashion for vintage clothes and for intense fashion sub-groups (steampunk, for instance) speaks of this desire to find experiences and places to belong that are real and have an authentic centre. There is a movement for craft and for artisan foods, beekeeping, craft beer and belongings – we want to know about the means of production. In a way this harks back to the Arts and Crafts movement of the nineteenth century and it too was looking for something that felt real and individually tailored. We are curiously still living in the shadows and preoccupations of our Victorian forebears.

In this yearning for the authentic there is a sense that the past might have something to teach us. Indeed, we need only to look at the fervour of youngsters with the green agenda to know that they love the world and the creatures in it, and we as a church ignore this at our peril. We have a lot to say about the beauty of the world and our role as co-sustainers of it. It amazes me that we don't welcome people's pets into church and pray for them and acknowledge the great impact they have on our lives. If only there had been the parable of the faithful dog or loving cat then things might be a great deal different today. We need to understand the things that people really care about, because we care about them too.

By not often acknowledging the creatures we share our planet with, church can seem overly locked into the world of ideas, without allowing seekers to taste God's beauty and abundance first. Or perhaps this might be better put by saying that, if seekers can see that what we already have points to God, then it's simply a continuation of their seeking to take a step towards him – or at least find out a bit more.

It was a technique that St Paul used in his own evangelism. He pointed out to the Athenians, who were inveterate seekers, that they were already seeking the unnamed God, but he could help take them a step further. He could help them name and know the God who was tantalisingly close and who already loved them.[5]

Despite the rise of science, many still have a sense of myth and legend and long for something that feels less rigid and mechanical than the lives they lead. Surely the incredible success of *Game of Thrones* (a sword and sorcery epic played without irony) says something about an appetite for something that is

not twenty-first century. The strength of Celtic rus-
ticity, along with its ancient credentials with a sense
of holy places, pilgrimage, the battle between good
and evil (supernatural) forces, plays very well with
the modern unchurched.

The worldview and created world of a TV epic like
Game of Thrones seem to prepare modern folk for
another kind of epic – the Celtic way. And when they
come across it, they are amazed that church has
anything like this to offer. As with the appreciation
of nature, we already have points of connection. We
have much more in common than people think, and
we can use this at least to start a discussion.

The ancient Celtic prayer for safety, from the Western Hebrides, seems to speak deeply into the heart
of modern unchurched folk. It could almost come
straight from the mouths of the rugged night watch
trying to keep the people of Westeross safe from the
White Walkers.

> Safeguard, O God, this household tonight, its
> persons, its means of life, its good name, deliv-
> ering it from death, from danger, from harm, and
> from the harvest of envy and hatred . . .[6]

This sense of needing protection in the face of a
very uncertain world is no less important today. In

a world where suicide bombers can attack places where young people hang out, there is a real understanding of how precious and fragile life is and the need for guarding. Just take a read of a regular British tabloid and the uncertainty we feel about the world is likely to spiral. Risks to health and wealth are apparently everywhere, and society's safety net seems very thin.

Neither does the prayer-poem duck what we face. Our good name is fragile. We want to be well thought of. There is danger from harm. We have to contend with envy and hatred. Indeed, these dread factors are being harvested all the time. It doesn't dodge what we face and much of that is a product of sin.

And this prayer uses the full armour of the poetic imagination. It begins with an image that appeals direct to the heart of any anxious person. Who could resist the offer of protection for their household? On a dark night we fear being burgled. We wonder what might happen at work during the week. We sometimes wonder if we might survive intact. Workplaces can be rough and remorseless and places of envy, hatred and game-playing. This prayer puts a cloak of protection upon the things we long for and know can be snatched away.

This works because it is such a surprising request. Yes, we ask God for all the big things and the traditionally holy things, but this simple invocation asks for the protection of our possessions. Home is a powerful idea for all of us. Home is more than bricks and mortar – it is a rock and a place we can be ourselves. Where better to be protected?

It isn't that we ditch what we have, but that this kind of prayer opens up a fresh avenue of spiritual development and connection.

We are not insulated from the old fears and forces and, in fact, many of us still experience them. Many of the regular people I speak to, many who never come to church, tell me about odd encounters with the supernatural. They describe encounters with a sense of evil and peril and I believe them.

I remember just before I first became a Christian. I considered myself a rationalist with a decent mind. I was a writer in the world of brands and business, living in West London. One evening my wife and I were sitting in our front room and we both experienced a sense of such evil that it scared us. We both felt the room go cold; we clung to each other and wondered what on earth was happening. It wasn't something you could call 999 about! After a while it passed, but it was visceral, and it was a bit disturbing.

Looking back, I am as sure as I can be that we had an experience with the forces of supernatural evil.

I find it interesting that it happened just before we went to church for the first time and months before our conversion experiences. It was just this kind of experience that is very, very common in our sophisticated, scientific and rational world. If we move out of the realm of the metropolitan then it seems that experiences of the 'other side' are all too common – which might explain why so many consult mediums and the like.

This is not superstition; of that I am sure. It is so important not to get sniffy about these experiences and say they come from ignorance. I do not believe they do for an instant. But if we get too mechanistic or propositional about faith, too concentrated on getting people to pray the one salvation prayer, do we not miss a chance to open a doorway into their lived experience and discuss the need for real protection?

St Cuthbert, the saint of the church at which I am vicar, had a huge sense of being assailed by demonic forces. Interestingly, Luther, father of the Reformation, had his own run-ins with the devil.

St Cuthbert, of course, shared this battle with all the Celtic saints. Their stories show that for the Celts the supernatural realm was alive and close and that they could trust God to be their shield. The Celts allow us to understand that, in the long dark night of the soul, we do not have to be alone.

Churched

Perhaps, though, Celtic spirituality also has something to offer us all? It is certainly true that I have
met many people on the evangelical spectrum who
love the way they do their faith but would like a
bit more time for reflection and quiet as well. But
it is out there and in the more evangelical wing of
the church. Eugene Peterson's poetic paraphrase of
the Bible, *The Message*, is a masterpiece.[7] Brooke
Fraser's beautiful worship and secular songs are full
of imagination and pack a punch.

But there are dangers and I, at least, have fallen vic-
tim to most of them. It is easy to feel we need to shop
around for the best preaching and the best worship.

We can become both over-intellectualised (just
try listening to a mammoth expository sermon)
or over-heatedly emotional (gold falling from the
rooftops in distant mega churches, people claiming
to regrow legs). These are caricatures, of course,
but there is room for a third space – at least as a
breather from the other stuff. And the Celts managed to produce both theologians of great stature
and passionate heartfelt prayers.

We are in need of a bit of poetry for the soul as much
as anyone else and we respond well when reminded

that God baptised the whole of creation and that he is close and in our daily lives.

On a theological level the Celts were totally Trinitarian. This is helpful and allows us to see God in the round. God is always, Father, Son and Holy Spirit. It seems, at least to me, that if we concentrate too much on one then we can at least lose a sense of balance.

This Trinitarian focus explains the Celtic love of community and their belief in hospitality. After all, what is the Trinity if it isn't a joyous community of love and creativity? All this is refreshing to many Christians who wonder where the rest of the Trinity went and want to think again about our God – three-in-one. As the ninth-century Welsh poem goes:

> Purely humbly, in skilful verse
> I should love to give praise to the Trinity,
> according to the greatness of his power.
> God has required of the host of this world
> who are his, that they should at all times,
> all together fear the Trinity.[8]

It is a good corrective and a help for us to hold the power of the Trinity in awe and holy fearfulness. The poet humbly asks that they could praise the Trinity in love. And that is a beautiful way to start any day.

And even all these centuries later there are still glimpses of Celtic ways in the Anglican Church – in Cranmer's rhythmic prose (designed to be heard as well as read), in the Anglican priest-poets like George Herbert and in the prayers for almost everything in the Book of Common Prayer.

This speaks of the Celtic way not being an odd and irrelevant import, but a whisper from our own Christian past. To many it feels like coming home. And who could not respond to a poem-prayer as honest and touching as the following?

> Take me often from the tumult of things into Thy presence. There show me what I am and what Thou hast purposed me to be. Then hide me from Thy tears.[9]

Anyone with an ounce of integrity is likely to say Amen to this.

4

Points of Connection:
Creation and Closeness

I want to see how Celtic spirituality can and does interact with evangelical church. So here are some key connection points between the Celts and their spirituality and modern churches and modern people. Some of these connection points act as ways of backing up traditional evangelical services and practices. Indeed, the Celtic way is ancient but very appealing to the modern mind as well.

The five connection points are:

1. Creation
2. Closeness
3. Covering
4. Creativity
5. Community.

God has baptised the whole of the created world

I receive an email from one of my tutors at Oxford. She helps me to frame my thinking and to see why the Celtic angle on creation is both a doorway to faith and offers an understanding of why we cannot truly be followers of Jesus and at the same time take the created world lightly. She points out that our Christian forebears were, in many ways, closer to the Bible because they were closer to the circumstances in which it was written. They depended on the natural world just as the Bible's authors did.

> They loved nature but they also respected it and were aware of their need to work with it rather than against it. It spoke to them of their Creator, God in his majesty and transcendence, but also his intimate nearness. Our western culture is disconnected from the natural world in so many ways. We have lost the rhythms of the seasons

and turn night into day, yet there is a deep long-ing to know God and an intuitive sense that the natural world can help us do so. With growing awareness of the seriousness of the ecological crisis, there is an added sense of urgency.[1]

My church is full of animal lovers, people who love their gardens, enjoy birdwatching and walks. It is per-haps no wonder then that they have taken to Celtic worship so well. They are delighted to realise that their love of the natural world is also a love for God and an act of gratitude on their part. It frees up a vast area of spirituality that has lain dormant – claiming something they love and care for as part of God's plan and purpose in their own lives. The Celtic Christians had a faith rooted in their everyday life and they were moved to praise, write poetry and songs and to share stories about the natural world they were so con-nected to. We can still have a longing for this connec-tion and our faith isn't shut out from it.

The Celtic way sees the whole created order as under God's care and love and as sharing in that goodness. They saw God revealed in creation. His creativity shone through in the beauty of nature and its seasonal rhythms.

From the tiniest insect to the stars in the distance, they are *all* part of God's goodness. The creation bears God's footprints. Nature is a blessing and also reveals God and his immense creativity.

This strikes such a deep chord with modern people. On my recent trip to the Edinburgh Fringe it was impossible not to notice the rage and anger that exists about subjects like the environment. Why should people be so unhappy? After all, they will be long dead before the chickens come home to roost. The only conclusion I can draw is that people have a deep love of our home planet and recognise that it is so beautiful that to ruin it would be the crime of all crimes. We have so much to offer here. Indeed we lead the way, very often. As Christians, we sometimes squabble about issues that, at least to many, seem to be of rank 2, rather than rank 1 importance.

The Celtic Christians have something to say to all of us. God is the beginning of all things and all things are part of the proclamation of his goodness. Gerard Manley Hopkins wrote: 'the world is charged with the grandeur of God'.[2] The Celts would have said 'Amen' to that. The birds, stars and sky were a tapestry with God's hands all over it. Everything under the sun somehow proclaimed God's goodness and the goodness of things.

This comes as a huge relief to modern people. The songs, verses and liturgies of the Celts are full of this appreciation of nature. This love of what we see about us, expressed so beautifully, is a very winning formula. The Celtic prayers revel in having Jesus at the centre. They never sideline him. They rejoice in the birds and sky and the sun. They reclaim them and help us to know why we worship God. The charge of nature worship is unjust and takes us away from the intrinsic godliness of the Celtic way. For the Celtic Christians nature was not scenery and it wasn't a goddess. They didn't separate nature and faith.

Maybe they were helped by spending so much time outdoors. They worshipped outdoors and worked outdoors. In our atomised and indoor lives and hefty church buildings we have sometimes closed ourselves off from the outdoor God.

A ninth-century Irish poet wrote:

> Let us adore the Lord
> Maker of marvellous works,
> bright heaven with its angels,
> And on earth the white-waved sea.[3]

As one reads more and more of the poems and prayers of the Celts one does not see pantheism, but a love for our home planet and the God who is revealed in all its beauty and complexity. One sees a deep reverence for the planet we share with our animal friends and a great outpouring of awe. But always this is shown as an expression of the divine and his vast and abiding creativity and animation of all that moves and lives on the planet.

It is interesting to note that two modern-day non-Christians have helped to reignite this awe. David Attenborough and Professor Brian Cox both bring the extraordinary beauty of the world and the cosmos into our living rooms. They simply shine with a sense of the beauty of the world, and their love of the planet and beyond is infectious and charming. Attenborough and Cox are tapping into our modern sense of awe and almost childish wonder at our planet. The Celts would have loved their programmes and shared the sense of wonder! But they would have taken a further step and claimed the extraordinary symmetry, patterns and wonder of creation for the Trinity. Many of us have had that sense of nature as a crucible of faith and a place of awe and love. Celtic spirituality makes the crucial link in the chain to the nature of God.

I think that our Celtic forebears would have wondered why we reflect only occasionally on the planet itself in our service and how we sometimes fail to draw the link between wonder and awe, nature and the God who is in it.

We have found that this dynamic is very powerful. Our Celtic service is able to draw from a huge range of blessings, poetry and prayer to celebrate the awe and wonder we all felt the first time we lay in the grass or looked up at the stars or had our first pet. The service reclaims this and adds a dimension that has been underplayed in decades past.

This is not pantheism, or New Age; it is baptism and the understanding that we are creatures among creatures and that we are all miracles of creation, sharing a planet with fellow miracles.

This overflowing of praise and appreciation is clear in so many of the prayers and poems of the period. They saw God as the king of all nature.

For our Celtic ancestors, animals were our friends, and when we lived in peace with them we were living out the cry of the most famous prayer ever written – Your kingdom come on earth . . . as in heaven. This is powerful medicine for us moderns who sense and see something wonderous in the animals we are friends with and those we admire.

And what's more, the Celts believed that animals actually ministered to us – bringing something of his divine love to their human friends. On the day before the great Saint Columba died, he had a premonition of his death. At that moment an old white horse that he knew well came over to him and laid his head on the saint's breast and wept. Anyone who has received the kindness of a cat or dog knows that animals have an extraordinary emotional intelligence. It is a gift from God.

Incidentally, the Celtic story is full of wonderful tales of the Celtic saints developing strong and lasting bonds with animals and forming deep friendships with them. It is interesting that in Mark's Gospel, Jesus, too, formed great bonds with animals during his time in the wilderness. Ian Bradley in *The Celtic Way* reports that St Serf had a pet robin and a lamb that followed him around and raised a dead pig to life. Ciaran was helped in the graveyard by a tame wild boar that helped him to dig the graves. In time he employed the boar as his servant. St Cuthbert had his life saved by wild animals on a number of occasions and the sea otters would dry and warm his legs when he had been praying all night in the water.

God in the everyday

While I was studying to be a priest I became friends with a local priest from a different denomination. We used to go into Oxford for coffee and enjoy walking in the University Parks. I responded to something of his calm way and think he liked my boyish enthusiasm for God.

I once asked him when he felt God's presence most keenly. I expected for him to say it was while presiding at Communion or on a high mountain. But no. He told me he was once listening to the radio while driving and that he had such a strong experience of God in the car that he almost pulled over. He was overwhelmed by just how close God was. This was a light-bulb moment for me. I began to wonder what other similar experiences were out there.

I took to asking all the visiting speakers at theological college about when they had most clearly met with God. It surprised me to hear of so many encounters that were so very ordinary. We heard about people who felt a profound sense of God when pushing their grandchildren on the swings. Another said that they felt God to be very close while changing into their kit to play a football match. Another felt the presence when listening to a favourite record. This closeness is a great spiritual gift and encouragement. It is a realisation that would have been second nature to the Celts. They expected God to show up wherever they were.

At college we did Bible study, prayer and modules on aspects of the faith, but it was these stories of encounter that truly stuck with me. For both seekers and Christians alike, the idea of a God who is thrillingly close is something that genuinely stirs the soul. I have one of those minds, though, that really wants to understand what it is like to meet the creator of everything in the everyday.

I have often felt God's presence in very ordinary moments. Sometimes it is just when I encounter the love and trust of another human being. At others, it is while going about my everyday life. God seems to be around as we have our morning toast and marmalade and that is a mind-boggling thought. Meeting God seems at once totally normal and beyond comprehension. I am sure that our Celtic forebears would have understood.

The Celtics had a strong sense of the miracle of everyday life, because God was so clearly in it. They turned this into celebration and song.

The Celts and closeness to God

For the Celts there was a strong sense that God was with them every step of the way in their daily lives. Their prayers for the everyday business of life are just as relevant today as they were then. And their sense of closeness is marked by a naturalness and familiarity of language.

For the Celts, daily life was made holy as they knew that God was with them close by in everything they did.

I will kindle my fire this morning
in the presence of the holy angels of heaven.[4]

I wonder how our faith lives would be transformed by these Celtic insights. On one level we are rather good at understanding the closeness of God, and in this we stand alongside our forebears. Our worship songs picture Jesus as a friend, our improvised prayers frequently call on Jesus to be close and we thrive on a sense of connection. The sense of God's closeness was one of the things that most amazed me when I first went to Pentecostal church as an adult. It is something that has never left me.

But where the Celts might have something to teach us, is in the location of God. Over the years many of my prayers have been deeply personal – a chat between God and me. I have frequently prayed for God to stand beside me – but very rarely have my prayers moved away from myself to the simple everyday world around. I might pray for a friend to be saved but I rarely honour God in my day-to-day life – in peeling the spuds, walking to the shop or stroking the cat. The Celtic Christians kept up a daily conversation with God, involving him in everything. He was their friend and he was in their lives and homes. It felt normal to chat to him about what they were doing – not just ask him for things.

The Celts ordained everyday life; it was pregnant with God. When they made the fire, they welcomed the angels to be with them in the piling of the wood and the lighting of the flame. They didn't pray for things in the way we do, perhaps. Or, to put it another way, they involved the saints, the angels and the Trinity in their everyday life quite naturally. And this sense of ordaining everyday life helped them to live simply within the rhythms of every day.

Holy moments

This is a useful antidote if we are tempted to look mainly for a sense of holiness in the big worship service on a Sunday. Again, I do want to be nuanced here. There is nothing better than a beautiful service and a worship band leading us into the presence of God. What we can learn, though, from our Celtic brothers and sisters is to broaden the places where we look for contact with our Lord.

By involving God in our prayers for and about our daily business and work we get a deep sense of the dignity of labour. It is almost as though God is with us in the work of our hands and, if this is so, we have to honour and value our co-workers and friends. Co-workers are to be respected as fellow workers, supported as part of a team and as equally made in God's image and doing God's work in the mundane tasks of the day. In this way the Celtic liturgy can help us to get a new perspective on work and our co-workers. I have often fretted about how we get God into the workplace. But the Celtic Christians would have looked at it differently, I think. They would have seen the act of honouring, supporting and encouraging their co-workers as a way of acknowledging that God is already there.

With this kind of material in a service, people tend to get a fresh insight into the scope, not just of God's love, but of his abiding presence. This may take them into a new depth of relationship and some thoughtful times wondering about the way they conduct themselves during the day.

Beginning, middle and end

And the Celts had a way of praying that had an economy of words combined with a sweeping scope. Often in the poems and prayers we see an understanding of God as close throughout our lives. The Celts hold together a sense of beginning, middle and end that is most helpful. As a modern-day Christian, I almost never pray about my death or think about the death of others. I have that sense of invincibility that the moderns share, coming from a world of hospitals and medicine and stable government and law – despite a pandemic.

But would our prayers be more enriching if we had a sense of our own mortality and need for God? If the peril of our fragile lives could whisper to us, we might have more of a sense of God the eternal sustainer of life, with us through death and beyond.

> But be thou thyself, O God of life, at our breast and behind us, a star and guiding from the beginning of life to its ending, through Jesus Christ our Lord.[5]

In some ways, our ancestors can teach us to pray – not to throw out what we already do but to add new variants and a new perspective. In this little poem/prayer we are encouraged to see God as the life companion we all need and to anticipate meeting with our Lord at the end of things. Seeing the great scope and economy of Celtic prayers can encourage us to aim for the same profundity and brevity.

But mainly it can encourage us to think about the end of our lives as well as the moment we are in. One day, each of us will know death. The plans we were making will be over and whatever busyness we were engaged in will be far less important than we thought it was. Thinking about it, the only time I have ever prayed with people about death is when they were actually near the end of their lives. My Celtic forebears teach me to get started much earlier and to acknowledge that for all of us death is as much a part of life as being alive itself.

If we frame our lives with the end and with what lies beyond, we can perhaps find new avenues of prayer and new insights into the way God is mighty and with us all the way.

For the journey

For most of us a journey is something to be got over. We rarely pray about our everyday journeys. But, surely, we miss something because of our blasé approach. The journeys we take seem very different from those of our Celtic Christian ancestors. They mainly travelled by foot and mainly on pathways. We have motorcars and aeroplanes and the like. Travel has become a function and not much more. Journeys are what we endure in order to get what we want and where we want.

The Celts had a whole range of beautiful prayers for journeys that we can adopt.

> Be my path this day with God, my path with Christ, my path with the Spirit, the three-fold trinity, all-kindly ho! ho! ho! All-kindly . . .[6]

Imagine if, on our way down to the tube station or bus stop, we were able to say a prayer like this. Accompanied by the kindly Trinity, we too might burst into a jolly laugh and begin to treasure our journeys as much as the destination.

True, waiting for a delayed train, crammed on to a tube or stuck in traffic we might not feel too jovial, but it must be worth a try. True that breaking into a Ho! Ho! Ho! might get us some very funny looks.

One of the influences of the Celts is to help us to slow down and notice what we have and what is around us.

God in partnership with us

Not many of us are farmers, but this charming little prayer helps us to imagine what it might be like to be one. Perhaps the point is that, although we aren't farmers, we can see in it a tenderness towards the animals the farmer is nurturing.

> Bless O God my little cow.
> Bless O God my desire;
> Bless Thou O my partnership,
> and the milking of my hands, O God.[7]

The Celtic insistence that God is in the little things of life helps to baptise these moments. We see the holiness of everyday living and that helps us to appreciate our lives all the more. The sense that God is everywhere and interested in everything is a very powerful motivator to keep on in the faith.

The prayer is on a human scale but acknowledges the great company of God. It has a tenderness and affection lacking in many a set-piece prayer. It also acknowledges our desires – our wants and dreams for things to do well, even if that's just milking the cow well. Although I love this poem, I also chuckle at a verse from Peter Ryder's playful song *Holy Columba*:

> There are high crosses rising in council house gardens and enough Celtic blessings for every tea towel. Computer consultants are waxing exultant at prayers to be said when they're milking a cow.[8]

Other Celtic poems also stress that our good desires matter to us and to God. In this we see a view of God as the encourager. Elsewhere we read:

> O Lord Jesus, grant us goodness, the goodness of the eye, the goodness of liking, the goodness of heart's desiring.[9]

It is a relief to know that seeing something beautiful is also good. This echoes the sentiment Keats expresses in his poem 'Ode on a Grecian Urn' that 'Beauty is truth, truth beauty'.[10] This prayer asks the Christ to help us to like the things and people around us and to treasure our dreams and desires. Christ, it seems, will tread softly on our dreams and that is no small blessing. How many of us have heard hurtful words about our likes and dreams – crushed by those who would see us trapped in tiny lives and ambitions?

Most touchingly, the cow prayer acknowledges a sense of mutuality – a partnership – between cow and farmer and perhaps between them both and God. The Celts relied on their animals and treasured them. Where would they have been without them? They were members of the family with great worth and were treated as honoured guests. Indeed, wild animals were also treated as guests and friends. They weren't simply something out there. They were creatures to be welcomed and blessed and to be little friends. The list of animal friends we see in Celtic literature is huge. St Cuthbert himself had a particular affinity with eagles. Others favoured flies, mice and frogs.

The prayer could have been so much blunter and, indeed, our prayers frequently are, as we pray for health and wealth. It could just be about helping us have a good day at work. But this lovely prayer seems to speak about flourishing and God in the everyday and how the work of our hands, or minds, has an innate dignity and value. And all that in just 24 words. It is poetry as well as prayer, and poetry always has the potential to move us and speak into the depths of who we are. The Celts appear to have been more poetry than prose people.

I have been known to babble from the front of the church. Sometimes my extemporised prayers have taken on a life of their own. Occasionally I have noticed people sleeping during one of my longer sermons. Our Celtic Christian brothers and sisters have a way of helping us to see something of the nature of God and how he works in words that are few and beautifully crafted. The message in this little poem/prayer could sustain a preaching series for a good number of weeks.

But, as importantly, it gives us a slightly different way of looking at the world, without denigrating all that is good about our own traditions.

There is a deep sense of the rhythm of the day, each step accompanied by God. So, from when we wake, wash, eat, work, play and sleep – we celebrate this sense of reassuring rhythm and God's presence. And there is a wealth of prayers acknowledging God's presence in all the milestones of life, birth, marriage, journeys, settling into a new house. The Celtic way rejoices in daily life, probably because that was what people had. They simply lacked the over-stimulation of today's world. They had rhythm, in the way that people at the time of Christ had the rhythms of daily life. We have lost touch with this and it is to our detriment.

But, of course, many evangelical churches have cottoned on to praying for people and their work, which is good. Some make sure they pray for people in their work and for the week to come. Others run *This Time Tomorrow* sessions during a service, when a member of the congregation comes up and explains their work and how God is with them, and the whole congregation then prays. This is a really encouraging development and helps congregations to link what happens on a Sunday with the rest of their lives. The Celtic sense of daily life can help both to cement this and to reiterate God's involvement in the nuts and bolts of life. It is reassuring that our ancient ancestors also went about their daily life – doing their work, caring for their families – and that they did this while praying and thanking God for every small detail.

As with so much of the Celtic pattern there are strong links to what evangelical churches already do.

It may be the old faith, but it is surprisingly contemporary in its application.

Just in this short introduction we can see how very appealing the Celtic way is to modern people with their rushed and hectic lives, grabbing lunch at their desks or on the move.

Those who have departed

The Celtic Christians had a great sense of the closeness of the saints and the disciples. There is a homely and intimate language that encourages us to see continuity between those who are living and those who have departed. Some may be uncomfortable with this, but it does chime with some deep feelings of closeness of the departed that many people experience.

An Orthodox priest and I were once talking about what happens when people die. I remember asking if he thought it wrong if we prayed to the dead, rather than for the dead. I remember his simple answer – 'if the dead are not there, why do they seem so close?' I am sometimes struck by a great sense of my wonderful father who died eight years ago. I can almost hear his voice and I sense him encouraging me from the sidelines. Rather than feeling a bit guilty about this, our Celtic Christian brothers and sisters would have found this completely normal. Perhaps we need to feel a bit less worried about going off the tramlines and relax a little.

This is a simple ancient fisherman's prayer:

Who are the group near to my helm?
Peter and Paul and John the Baptist:
Christ is sitting on my helm,
making guidance from the wind to the South.[11]

Even if we see this as a bit fanciful, it is certainly interesting. If our imagination were a bit more pliable, would it not be possible to feel the presence of the saints in our daily lives? I sometimes hope that this might be possible.

Perhaps we who are travelling in our own little metaphorical boats can also look to the company of the great apostles. We may be surrounded by a great cloud of unseen witnesses, those who have gone before, and we would do well to take the encouragement they offer.

And maybe, the Celts and their great connection to nature is much more contemporary than we give it credit for. Dave Bookless, Anglican priest and writer on creation tells me.

Celtic Christianity is sometimes spoken about as if it was something a bit quaint and strange because it took creation seriously. I would argue, rather, that the Celts were simply living out the normal Christian life, and it is we modern, dualistic, individualistic Christians who are abnormal. The Gospel, the Good News of Jesus Christ is about a restoration of all the relationships broken by sin and alienation from God. It therefore involves a triple conversion: to God in Christ, to 'the other' – reconciliation with our neighbour and especially those who we see as different or alien, and thirdly a conversion to the earth. It is our conversion to the earth, from which we were made and to which we will return, and after which we were named 'Adam', that has been sorely neglected in modern western Christendom. The Celts, along with the early church, St Francis, and Christians in many other cultures – particularly indigenous ones – have always recognised our complete dependence upon nature, and that God speaks to us through two books: nature and scripture. We only need to read the Psalms, or the Sermon on the Mount, to see that creation spirituality is the norm for the people of God.[12]

5

Points of Connection: Covering

Covering – the desire for God's protection and blessing

In the Pentecostal church where I began my journey of faith, and which I still love and admire, we would often pray for God's covering, his protection, with a sense of real and present evil close to us. We knew that there were forces out there that wanted to trip us up and challenge our faith. We had a sense of the supernatural, and it is a sense shared by many others. We were not immune to the many dangers of life – but then who is?

This prayer is as relevant today as it ever was.

> I lie in my bed
> As I would lie in the grave,
> Thine arm beneath my neck,
> Thou Son of Mary Victorious.[1]

There is something muscular about the Christ with his arm beneath our neck, holding us up in the face of the enemy. We can picture this. Christ's strong arm around us, holding us up, keeping us breathing. And the picture becomes even more vivid and drawn with admirable economy. He is Mary's son. He is on a human scale and we get a sudden feeling for his family and the relations there. We picture Christ the son, the boy who helped his dad in the family business, doted on by his mum. The son his mum worried about and would do anything for.

The 'Son of Mary', the sustainer of all, is there to protect us. But from what? The writer of this prayer seems oppressed and anxious. We have perhaps all felt like this at times. His bed seems cold as the grave, he or she feels half-dead. Who hasn't had the early hours' feeling of loneliness and terror? That great Bard of Manchester, Morrissey specialised in a certain grim realism. In one of his lyrics he laments that the sink has frozen up and his home feels like a grave. We've all been there.

Who knows why the writer of this poem felt so grave-like? But there are times when something evil seems to lurk and times when we feel as scared as children on their own in their rooms at night. The Celts painted vivid pictures of the Christ as the one who is unafraid – the son of his mother who has his arm around us.

Many modern people have experiences of fear and supernatural evil. They may not use the language of cosmic battle, but that is what they are experiencing. There is a sense of existential evil that many can attest to. And we can be assailed not just in spooky situations and places. Even in the midst of an ordinary modern day we can suddenly become aware of something uncanny pressing into our consciousness.

Celtic spirituality is well-versed with the idea of battling with evil forces. Interestingly, this sense of spiritual warfare is at the heart of a key area of doctrine for many charismatic churches – another point of connection between Celtic spirituality and the modern Church. Or we might call this an open door through which the Celtic liturgies and prayers can come to our aid. The link is so beautifully close that it isn't hard to incorporate some of what the Celts have to offer. The Celtic way managed both to be very sensitive to the forces of evil and to herald creation as something that is friendly. So the sense of peril never overcomes the great overriding sense of optimism that our forebears cultivated.

As well as experiencing a sense of supernatural oppression and attack, many of us feel anxious – both overtly and in subtle ways about our families and those we love. We know how fragile life is and how evil can come our way. We fear what might befall us and we feel helpless.

The Celts had a deep understanding of supernatural forces, the fragility of life and the power of God and his mighty angels to protect us. Their sense of cosmic battle would have been matched by their knowledge of the sheer fragility of life. Few made it through to old age. The plague was a constant danger, there were no antibiotics and even a simple illness could quickly become serious and the person die. They lived with both their own mortality and the sense of threat.

But this fragile world and sense of vulnerability surely whisper to us today. We live in a time when our young people, especially, are showing signs of tremendous strain – from exams, social media bullying and body insecurity, to name but three sources of stress. One imagines that this unholy trinity would have been rather alien to our Celtic forebears, but the end result is the same. Insecurity. Or to put it another way, people ask from where does our help come?

An ancient Highlands' prayer asks this of the Trinity:

> Be our sanctuary . . . shielding our whole life, this day and this night, from hate and harm . . . henceforth and forever.[2]

The shield is a powerful image, and notice that the writer invokes it through the whole of life, not just for the moment at hand. He draws an interesting parallel between hate, harm and evil. A deadly alternative trinity that can trip up even the wisest. It feels curiously modern, as do many of the poems and prayers we have from our ancient past.

Indeed, there is a strong sense in much Celtic material that the Trinity is a bastion and shield, a comforter and protector. In 'St Patrick's Breastplate' it is literally a suit of armour to help combat the twin evils of despair and fear.

Used in a Celtic service, especially on a stormy Sunday evening when people are beginning to feel melancholy and vulnerable, prayers of protection can be very effective. People have a visceral sense of threat (as I say, anxiety is at a record high) and we are well placed to use the wisdom of the ancient Celts to proclaim God's protecting hand. Despite all the 'certainties' we now have, we oddly feel just as uncertain as ever.

The Celts would regularly act out encircling a person or space to mark an area protected by God. They had a strong sense of the threat of the devil and demons. Although modern people don't express this sense in these words, there are few of us who don't remember times when we have felt ourselves in the presence of embodied evil. Many of us have had chilling experiences and many have felt captured by powers and forces beyond our control. Some of these are given expression in addictions of many kinds.

The Celts had a strong sense of God the protector in all situations. Their acknowledgement of the human condition and our vulnerability rings many bells today.

We need to understand the way the Celtic people understood the Cross and the atonement. For them the Cross was not so much God paying a ransom for our sins, as the defeat of the very real powers of evil both here and in the heavenly realms. Christ was a superhero who could, did and would take on his and our enemies.

Christ's death and resurrection dealt a fatal blow to these demonic forces, although they still have much power to do harm. But in Christ as victor we have a strong and reliable protector. The Celts had a militaristic view of the Christian spiritual life. We are under attack by the enemy, we have the protection of our baptism and our Jesus.

The world may look all scientific and consisting of only what we can see and touch, but even in the most rational mind there lies some deep part that knows that we are under threat and that the forces that line up against us are persistent and all too real. Without unduly scaring people, the Celtic service is a place to articulate these fears and gain the beautiful reassurance that we have a protector big enough to take on all comers. We are not alone in wanting to cry out to God for protection. We live in a time when we are encouraged to shield the vulnerable from a deadly disease. The Celts often used the language of God as the ultimate shield. And our Celtic forebears made full use of one particular image: putting on the breastplate of protection – armour to withstand the attacks that will inevitably come. And the prayers were very specific. Try this from *The Breastplate of Laidcenn*:

> Protect my spine and ribs and their joints,
> Back, ridge and sinews with their bones;
> Protect my skin and blood and kidneys,
> The area of the buttocks, nates and thighs.[3]

This prayer doesn't just show an impressive knowledge of anatomy, it also gives a gloriously earthy picture of God's protection over all our parts. And when we read it, we are opened up to a new sense of how wonderful our bodies are because God made them and that even the parts we rarely mention are full of holiness and the care of creation. This is a prayer that should be standard reading for us who tend to live too much in the mind. I have no idea what one's nates are, by the way, but will leave that up to you, dear reader, to find out.

But if this ancient prayer can draw our attention to the embodiedness of our life experience then it is doing us a good service. The Celts wanted God to protect everything that mattered and, for them, in an age that relied on spells, runes and potions, God was a much more reliable bet than anything else on offer.

The trick, of course, is not just to pray it, but to believe it. When we get that sense that God is there and that he cares for us and that he is the great protector, then it tends to put things into perspective.

I wonder what our breastplate prayer would be today? Perhaps it would be less about physical things – we have painkillers and the like to get us through the day. Yes, we fear the dread illnesses – dementia and cancer. But we may need some specific protection against, for instance, a bullying boss, an attack on Facebook or a broken family situation. The list would be endless and we can take the template of the breastplate prayer and make it our own.

Long before I was a Christian, I found myself one day in Southwark Cathedral. I can't remember why, but I was feeling oppressed and anxious. This was a common state that I was experiencing. I think the pressures of business and being a father were weighing heavily on me. I simply wasn't quite sure where to turn.

I went up during the Communion and asked the bishop for a blessing. I think this was the first time I'd even seen a bishop and it certainly had novelty. But there was more to it than this. I was tapping into a powerful, ancient impulse: to turn to the church and turn to God when all seems uncertain.

I don't remember what it was, but I do remember feeling absolutely wonderful afterwards! My life didn't feel very blessed, and hearing the beautiful ancient words of a godly blessing was very welcome. I was one of many who needed to experience a prayer of blessing and protection and now, as a priest, being able to pray these over people is one of the great honours of the office. Sunday by Sunday, people want to be prayed for because they feel vulnerable.

Many of the Celtic words of blessing are mini works of art – beautiful literary creations. This is one we use at our service. We don't know where it came from but it engenders a deep sense of connection. It captures a sense of connection to the earth and to God and to the longing for peace.

> May the blessing of light be on you – light without and light within.
> May the blessed sunlight shine on you like a great peat fire,
> so that stranger and friend may come and warm himself at it.
> And may light shine out of the two eyes of you,
> like a candle set in the window of a house,
> bidding the wanderer come in out of the storm.
> And may the blessing of the rain be on you,
> may it beat upon your spirit and wash it fair and clean,
> and leave there a shining pool where the blue of Heaven shines,
> and sometimes a star.[4]

I challenge anyone with a love of words and a sense of poetry in their soul not to be moved by such a thing as this. There is more to come about the creativity of a Celtic service, but this is just a taster of the riches on offer.

And the Celts had blessings for all kinds of everyday things – for the chickens' eggs to hatch, for the sheep to behave, even for taking a bath. Translated into today's everyday happenings, we need blessings for our commuting, our safety online and all manner of other modern things.

Our experience is that people marvel at the God who can bless and protect. People have a sense of awe when hearing about angels and saints. Many non-Christians have had angelic encounters. This is a chance to help them see where angels fit in and to put their trust in Jesus who is their boss.

A unique twist

There is a subtle difference in the kind of prayers the Celtic Christians prayed and that twist may be a useful way of breaking one of the prayer-blocks many of us suffer from. We wonder, perhaps in our modesty or in response to Christ's entreaty to take up our crosses and follow him, whether and how we should pray for ourselves. It seems almost selfish.

And indeed, the water has been muddied by the unwelcome growth of 'health and wealth' praying and ministries.

Calvin Miller, in his book *The Path of Celtic Prayer*, helps us to see how the Celtic Christians prayed. He points out that their prayers would often be framed thus: 'God, only while I live can I serve you, so please protect and extend my life.'[5]

6

Points of Connection: Creativity and the Poetic Imagination

One small step

It is my contention that, had anyone other than Neil Armstrong been the first man on the moon, we would by now have been building communities on it, space travel would have been an everyday reality and NASA would have been the most powerful organisation on earth. What is still science fiction might have been everyday science fact.

I say this slightly flippantly, but I believe it to be true. The reason we stopped manned flights to the moon and our cosmological ambitions became strangled at birth is because we heard about the moon and its wonders from a scientist. Armstrong, for all his calm and admirable character, was never able to summon up the words to inspire us with what he saw. At least he wasn't able to describe the experience when he was the spaceman who had returned to earth.

Had he been a poet rather than a scientist then perhaps he could have captured for us what the moon meant and how seeing our planet from afar was a thing of such wonder that no person who had seen it could ever be the same again. Had a poet addressed us, we would have had our hearts on fire and becoming space-travellers might have been the great destination of us human beings.

It is interesting that, when NASA put teams together to crack the big scientific problems that existed in order to *get* a person on the moon, they used teams that included both scientists and the odd poet. But that was as far as the poets got a look-in, which is a great shame.

Poetry is life, because it opens us up to new realities using that most precious of things – language. Poetry helps us to see the world in a new way and that newness is a door to spiritual growth and the antidote to staleness.

When we stop using poetic language about God and his works and his creation then we have a narrower definition of the infinite being.

Perhaps the greatest challenge is how to live a little more like poets. Of course, we need to start with an appreciation of what the poets have to offer – especially in a world that seems to be awash with fake news, messages selling us things and an overload of data that just needs interpreting.

To rediscover the power of poetic language we need to appreciate the poets among us and nurture them and their talent.

The poet and the prophet

Walter Brueggemann's *Hopeful Imagination: Prophetic Voices in Exile* is surely one of the most powerful explanations of the role of poetry in the religious experience and the changing of society.[1] His work focuses on the prophetic books of Jeremiah, Ezekiel and Isaiah but what he says has relevance well beyond these texts. He makes some bold claims for poetry and how it actually works.

Brueggemann's thesis is that poetry is crucial because it allows us to understand newness and to do something new as a result of its insights. Unlike a manifesto that simply says what *will* be done, poetry brings about newness by picturing it in language that allows us to see things anew.

Poetry is unsettling and refreshes our sense of the world. It does this through metaphors (which expand language rather than reduce it) and picture language and the use of rhythm and form. What's more, poetic language tends to wear out a lot less quickly than prose or information language. When it comes to metaphor and image, each generation will take them on anew and imbue them with fresh insight and meaning.

To the Celtic writers a stony path might be a metaphor for the difficulty of finding God on a dangerous journey. To us it might speak into the flintiness of modern life. A ship on a tempestuous ocean might be a simple description of a daily reality to our forebears, but to us it speaks of tempestuous lives in a frantic world.

Poetry is of course a great challenge to any church, church leader or preacher. Poetry is the language of metaphor and pictures and uncertainty. Poetry is more provisional, and a church that wants to be more poetic must take a risk that poetry might shake us out of some certainties. Poets have always seemed mad, bad and dangerous to know.

I have heard preachers who pick up their Bible, show it to the congregation and then say things like 'This is a manual for life. The answer to everything is here.' But what if the Bible is also poetry and that there is mystery here too and that when we pray and write liturgy we add new poetry that can challenge us in a less prosaic way? Again, it isn't either/or.

God comes to life in poetry because poetry is free to press speech to the limit and allow all that he is to come through. As Brueggemann says, 'I suspect that we lose vitality in ministry when our language of God is domesticated and our relationship with God is made narrow and predictable.'[2]

I longed to hear more poetry from the front at church. Or to put it more bluntly, I longed to use more poetry from the front. As ever, when things seem a bit wrong, its best always to 'start with me'. It was while reading some of the poems and prayers of our Celtic ancestors that I began to realise with a burst of excitement that this was possible.

Poets have access to language that can be passionate and dangerous and surprising and this in turn allows us to be surprised by God and all he is and has made.

Brueggemann offers markers of what makes a poet – and each is amply lived out in the poetry and prayers of our Celtic forebears. We might also add that each is also sadly lacking in most evangelical churches as they expand upon and sing about their faith.

1. The poet does not offer advice. That is the job of others. Poets try to surprise, add nuance and stimulate us. They want us to re-experience the world through using different images and metaphors to help us to see things anew. We see the world anew with poetry and that helps us to feel more in contact with God.
2. Poets use language that doesn't wear out quickly. We can reread a poem many times and still find new things in it. Poems thrive on ambiguity. Poetry leaves gaps. Poets push us to think about the world.
3. Poets transform our imaginative capacity rather than give us an ethics lecture.

Transforming imagination

I well remember when I first read E. E. Cummings' poem 'who knows if the moon's a balloon'.[3] It is not a Celtic poem but it was for me an object lesson in the power of poetry. And the more I read it the more

I began to see connections with the Celts. Cummings had an interesting way with capitalisation – he resisted the tyranny of capital letters, searching for something sinuous and free.

His poem is about freedom and love and what it is to break free from the gravity of our lives. It pictures a fresh reality and asks us to wonder about the power of journeys into the unknown.

In the poem, two lovers board a mysterious balloon set for a mysterious and beautiful city. I was simply so excited by it that I hardly knew what to do with myself. I was going through a particularly weighed-down period in my life, so the image of a balloon was something I aspired to. I wanted lift-off. Like many others, I had seen hot-air balloons and always found the sight cheerful and stirring.

The language of the balloon was very powerful to me. But as a poem it has an air of mystery. It's an odd image but it speaks of something beautiful and spontaneous. The balloon ride on offer helps us to soar away and we glimpse the steeples and houses and clouds, and finally we reach a city which nobody has ever visited.

What a poem it is. You could read a pile of books about being in love, you could understand the way love has an impact on us, but this poem with its strange, pretty people and mysterious lovers' city says more about the mystery of falling head-over-heels in love than all of that put together. The poetic imagination adds something quite magical to the kind of banal statements we often make about falling in love.

But what might the Celts have made of it – apart from commenting on its odd punctuation? I wonder if they might see it as a classic story of pilgrimage and claimed it as a poem of their own. They would surely have loved the images of nature and the rhythm of the piece and seen the city the balloon was heading to as the great city of God.

In *The Path of Celtic Prayer*, Calvin Miller acknowledges one particular Celtic saint as his hero. As I have said, Brendan was the great Celtic navigator; he was also the great wanderer and pilgrim.

Miller recounts how Brendan was lured into his great and fantastic voyage over the sea by Barinthus, a friend at the monastery. Barinthus had told Brendan the story of an amazing land, a story told to him by his grandfather. It was a land full of flowers and precious stones. Brendan wanted to go there and meet those who lived there in such holiness. He wanted nothing more than to travel and he and his companions did so in his little home-made boat. At first, they battled the elements and were on the point of being overwhelmed. Then Brendan told his companions to stop rowing and take down the sail. They were going to trust to the will of God as to where they landed – his winds and his sea.

The seekers in E. E. Cummings' poem were following in the steps of the great Celtic saint, even if the poet didn't know it. They too were searching for a land of flowers and they knew other ways than onwards.

The following prayer-poem is attributed to St Brendan. Those balloon adventurers in Cummings' poem could have prayed it with great sincerity. It is a poem that could be prayed by any modern person who feels a bit trapped and would like an adventure, who values the act of seeking and knows what it is to be tossed about by personal storms.

It rings down the centuries and is nothing less than a gift. It has all the hallmarks of poetry that Brueggemann highlights. A preacher could preach a whole sermon series on the need to let God be God, to step out in courage and confidence into his guiding and to discover the leader within; but this short blaze of poetic genius does it in a way that is so winning that we all feel ready to sign up to be on the tiny boat with the ancient saint.

Help me to journey beyond the familiar
and into the unknown.
Give me the faith to leave old ways
and break fresh ground with You.
Christ of the mysteries, I trust You
to be stronger than each storm within me.
I will trust in the darkness and know
that my times, even now, are in Your hand.
Tune my spirit to the music of heaven,
and somehow, make my obedience count for You.[4]

Just as we hurtle to the end of the poem another joy
awaits us. St Brendan asks that his spirit might be
tuned to the music of heaven. And with this we hear
the heavenly choirs singing and we think about how
music is so central to us. But it isn't a set of orders.
Indeed, the tiny, and easily missed, provisional 'and
somehow' adds a beautiful level of humility. Cannot
we all feel the exasperation at our own stubborn
hearts and flimsy efforts at obedience?

This great saint has left us a poetic jewel and it is one
among many that help us to think about our journey
with God a bit differently. It isn't that the nuts and
bolts of our services have to change – the passionate
talks, music and praying – it's just that we might find
room somewhere for the voice of an ancient saint
who once took his life in his hands, made a small
boat and let God do the driving.

Loving poetry and God

Poetry opens up doors for us and, however often I read this poem, each time I do so it feels as if I have never read it before. The language does not dry up or become clichéd – which is surely quite a feat when writing about young love.

Many of us have poems that mean a lot to us. I grew up loving Keats and Wordsworth and still do to this day. As a schoolboy, a trip to Keats' house was so magical that I can still remember the whole day and the sense of wonder at being in close proximity to this great poet. The language of Shakespeare is a potent and heady companion. If you are of a more modern vintage than me then there will be modern poets and poetry that will have spoken into your lives. But it is interesting how prose, film and music often date, while poetry (at least some of it) stands the test of time.

The charismatic church I started with was brilliant at using film clips, music, drama and sometimes painting to add depth and flavour to services. We had an openness to the creative arts.

Worship songs can be both pop *and* poetry. Some of these chants are very powerful and affecting. We can build on this and encourage a flowering of the poetic imagination, and that means encouraging the poet's way of looking at the world which produces the poetry.

Some folk are prose people. The Bible has much prose within it and much of that is amazing and wonderful. It is also a book of stories, poems and histories – among other things. We can combine both. But the knack may be to start thinking and praying and writing like the poet.

Poets can help us see the unseen, and poetry can open us to wonder and fresh ways of seeing the world. The interesting thing is that poetry can stand the test of time because each generation imbues a poem with their own cultural references, insights and connections. So when we read a Psalm, though we live in a very different world, because it is poetry we can adapt it and live in it so that it belongs to us as well.

I long for a mega-church experience that involves poetry – and that could be beautifully constructed liturgy or blessings. It is as though we have come adrift from our poetic moorings and we are perhaps the poorer for it.

Which brings us to the world of Celtic Christians and the fragmentary poems and prayers they have given to us. Many were collected centuries after they came into life by social anthropologists recording and writing down poems that had been passed down through the ages. But we do have some original sermons and prayers and blessings. They are a great treasure but we will only ever have a half-measure of what it was like to be a Celtic Christian. So we should always be careful not to think that they had the answers to everything.

But the poetic imagination of our Celtic brothers and sisters opens up a new vista on the world and the way we and God operate within it. This is one of the treasures on offer to modern-day Christians and our experience is that it is an easy bridge to cross.

A way of looking at the world that values creativity

There has been much more awareness in recent years from the evangelical church for the need to value the creative side of life and work.

The church is doing great work understanding about and being more creative and realising that a love of the Word doesn't mean that we can't be creative as well and welcome paintings, films, novels and other expressions of creativity and imagination.

But whatever the case, the ancient Celts' deep and abiding creativity reaches out to a modern non-Christian world that wonders why churches aren't more imaginative. The flowering of the Celtic way was accompanied not just by a valuing of creativity in the service of God but by some extraordinary artistic achievements.

This creativity is seen today in the hundreds of beautiful standing crosses, in illuminated books and in many of the songs and chants that have been passed down through the generations. Those crosses, Ray Simpson in *Exploring Celtic Spirituality* muses, were markers on the battlefield of spiritual warfare.[5] Perhaps each was put up to mark a particular victory against the powers of evil.

For those of us who get a bit fed up with leaden worship songs, over-long services and formulaic preaching, the Celts offer a window into a Christian world that is layered and that marshals both beauty and poetic precision to worship God.

Another way of putting this is to say that the Celts valued the power of the imagination and had a love of language and image that brings their worship to life. Ian Bradley makes the interesting observation that faced with the twin dangers of an over-intellectualised faith or an over-emotional one, the Celtic approach that is rooted in the imagination offers a way out.[6]

The Celts painted pictures in words and music and these still have great resonance and potential. Bradley says that we are past the age of innocence of the Celts. We cannot ever fully inhabit their animated world. But we can at least use their poems and prayers, songs and works of art.

The poems and prayers of the Celts are powerful because they use imagery, metaphor and symbolic language. They take the language of nature and peril and make it reflect our inward battles and perils.

> Seasons come and seasons go
> Tide streams ebb and tide streams flow,
> Father Son and Holy Ghost.
> Fill the days and cleanse the coast.[7]

In this little prayer we bring together the seasons of our own lives with the seasons around us. The prayer to cleanse the coast also talks metaphorically about all that needs cleansing within ourselves. It works on a number of levels – and in an age when our coasts are awash with plastics it has a resonance for us in these not so natural times. Notice too how it holds together the Trinity and sees it at the heart of the deep seasonality of life – something many of us only become aware of as we get past our middle years.

The ancient Highland prayer of blessing is a little masterpiece:

> May God shield us by each sheer drop, may God keep us on each rock-path, may the Spirit fill us on each bare slope, as we cross hill and plain.[8]

The image of the sheer drop jumps out at us – many of us have felt that moment of vertigo as we look over the precipice. We no longer carry shields, but we all understand that we might need one from time to time. Even if we live in a city, the picture of the rock-path is vivid and the bare slopes are a reality. Perhaps our modern readings show how much we tend to psychologise everything – although in the absence of rock paths in our cities there may be a good reason. For those of us who feel trapped in our tiny houses, the glimpse of hill and plain gives us a lungful of something wholesome.

> Watch over us, O thou God of the moon,
> Shed down on us thy lovely light,
> The darkness of evening is here too soon
> If with thy presence it be not bright.[9]

And here again we get the marker of the poetic imagination – letting us see afresh and freeing God from the constraints our dull language places on him. We worship the God of the moon – I had never thought of him like that. It is helpful because I see the moon most nights and I can now associate God with this. We love the idea of his lovely light and we all feel that darkness descends too soon. It also has that realism that lets us see things more clearly – we all lack a bit of God's brightness at times.

Each is a little jewelled work of art, using delicate language and images. And there are so many other examples. It comes as a shock to modern folk brought up on a diet of regular evangelical church to find that such riches exist. What's more, they offer a theology that is not at odds with what most churches teach.

Incorporated into your church, they can do nothing other than add new depths of encounter with God and encourage poets and writers and painters and filmmakers to see that they can use their own gifts to worship God. Read slowly and with time to contemplate the words, they can create a spiritual snowball effect.

Good poetry can actually be distinguished from bad relatively easily. Good poetry has an ability to apply to different generations. Each generation can take it and use the images and metaphors anew, to help the poetry speak into the lives of new communities.

The prayers and blessing and verses of the Celts have lost none of their power and indeed manage to speak into our own struggles and sense of awe and wonder in a world the original writers could never have imagined. They are full of hope and a gritty earthiness that helps us to see that God is in the everyday as well as the heavens. They are full of life.

When I first went to church I was amazed at the vibrancy I found. My only other experience of church had been being forced to go, in order to be in the Scouts. The service was interminable, the church was cold and I hated the music. I couldn't wait to get home. I had in my mind that church was boring and for old people.

Many years passed and I was invited to attend a service at a friend's church. I thought I'd go. The church was Pentecostal in flavour, had an amazing worship band and preaching that was relevant, funny and deep. I simply could not believe it. I had to go back.

Before the service I had been complacent about God. I had lost the knack of being happy with my life and had no one to say thank you to for the many blessings I had been showered with. I felt that my own creative edge had been blunted and began asking the kind of question that boils down to – isn't there more to life than this?

I became a believer in that church and I became a person of faith, hope and love. I have not left all this behind and I do not in any way look back with anything but great gratitude for what happened. I still love this kind of experience and this kind of church.

But the poetry of the Celts – the poetic imagination – has simply added another dimension to my faith and my awe towards God. It has added another string to my bow because it helped me reconnect with a way of looking at the world that I thought I had lost. It helped me to love poetry again and the way that poets think. It re-engaged my passion for social action and helped me to see that God is a bit of a mystery as well.

7

Points of Connection: Communities

We live in a world that is isolating and lonely. Research has shown that Britain has the highest levels of loneliness in the developed world and that London is the loneliest place within this country.[1] Loneliness is a modern scourge to which none of us is immune.

Whatever we have *now* in terms of being surrounded by loved ones could become a very different picture. Within a few doors of every church in the land there will probably be a person who does not see a living

soul all week and who does not know how they can
go on.

It is quite shocking. We have a society in which loneliness, atomisation and lack of community are being
experienced on an industrial scale.

The Celtic Christians took a high view of community. They lived in close proximity to people they
knew and cared for. Their village communities were
tight-knit and put together in concentric circles. They
would know the people who lived around them and
share in the stories of their lives. They would care
for those who were sick and stick together in good
times and bad.

Their model of community was the eternal Trinity.
The kind of loneliness that people experience today,
the sense of atomisation, may have been well beyond the experience of people in ancient society. I
wonder if they might be shocked at our callousness.
Perhaps, though, the coronavirus pandemic has
helped us to understand that without community
we actually have nothing.

For the Celts, as for people in Jesus' time, the mutual support and love of a community was a holy
duty as well as second nature. And there is a deep
resonance here with us as modern people and the

challenge of being church in a world which places such competing demands on people.

We long for the kind of community that seems to be a thing of the past. We long for something that is authentic and that enfolds us in the lives of others. As parish churches, we are ideally suited to be the bringers of community – the glue that holds people together. This kind of vision has a very Celtic feel to it. We can learn from the Celtic passion for community and the organic way that they loved and worshipped together.

If moderns want authentic community and are already looking for it, how can church be the bringer of this? How can we be more than just a Sunday exercise?

Belong then believe – the Celtic way

There may have been a time when simply stating propositional truth was a sensible evangelistic tactic. You preach the word in season and out of season, people make a commitment to Jesus and they become regular members of church. Bingo! When we read the stories of heroic preachers like George Whitefield and Charles Spurgeon it seems that simply delivering a sermon could lead to huge results.

Even if we doubt this, the pressure to deliver truth is still very real. We think of Billy Graham and his mass crusades, with people coming down to the front on the strength of a talk to give their lives over to Jesus. The truth seemed to have potency; I believe that it still does. But . . .

On a recent trip to Edinburgh I visited a church on the Royal Mile. Just reading the interior architecture told such a story. The church had no adornments, no altar, no stained glass. Instead, it had a huge elevated 'throne' from which the preacher was to help us to sit under the authority of the Word.

But what of today's reality? In an era of suspicion about information and authority and the constant shouting of 'fake news', why should our truth be any more relevant than any other truth? There is a mistrust of narratives that claim absolute truth – that, of course, doesn't mean that this truth narrative is not true! It is just that propositional truth is a hard product to sell. Or perhaps we might say that simple propositional truth is under pressure and that it is accepted best when accompanied by action – namely, love and care.

People are looking for something that is authentic and there is nothing more authentic than a community that cares for each other and feels like family. In our isolated society the realisation that there is a place we can call home is liberating and deeply attractive. In the US series that model of longing was a bar in Boston called Cheers – a place where everybody knew your name.

Perhaps building belonging and community is a way of establishing that God loves people and is a way of growing church. It isn't an either/or – it's a both/and. Preaching faithfully and orthodoxly is a great privilege and a gateway to the mind of God. Community on its own lacks depth if not backed by truth and truthfulness.

In Celtic Britain, in the years after the Romans had left and before the Roman Church began to reassert itself a few centuries later, there sprang up communities that helped this nation with its new invaders to discover the faith. These communities were sometimes monasteries – places of education, healing, learning, work and prayer with an open-door policy. They were also places of new technologies and entrepreneurship. New technologies such as the first tidal mill were established at monastic communities in Ireland. These were museums of the faith – they were exciting, modern and encouraging communities. Places you came to be fed in mind and spirit.

The Celtic pattern established by St Patrick in Ireland was based on monasteries which were communities rather than the Roman Church's diocesan structure.

At the heart of the Celtic way was the creating, sustaining and celebrating of community. The whole community worshipped together and they were interdependent in so many ways. And as the Vikings began raiding and tearing communities apart, they had to cling together for protection as well.

Communities of joy

The Celts believed in feasting and community events and that is a spirit that is very winning in our atomised world. Reading poems and prayers about community and feasting and joy is a very powerful affirmation to our modern guests that we are allowed to be happy and attached to other people in a purposeful community of love.

Feasting and celebrating brings community together. We tend to do this at big events in our nation's history. We have street parties for royal events and at millennia, but not so much otherwise. For the Celts, hospitality and celebration were part of the rhythm of life. During the coronavirus pandemic, we have had to be away from church and apart. When we get together again, I think we will all fancy a party and will be deeply relieved that we can be social. The Celts would have understood.

I have been in churches that charge people a few pence for a poor mug of coffee after the service. My friends, give the coffee away for free. What's more, provide the best coffee money can buy in beautiful mugs. Give away cakes and biscuits and encourage a sense of beautiful abundance.

Our Celtic forebears might have encouraged us to do a bit more feasting and singing and to create genuine communities of young and old. They did not really differentiate between church and life – the same feasting mentality reigned in each.

I wonder what they would have made of segmented church communities that aim only at, say, university students or potential young leaders. I think they might have struggled to understand them and wondered why young and old were not learning from each other.

The Celtic Christians offer us an invitation to celebrate and to feast and be full of all the joy that makes life worth living. That is surely a winner, especially when so many of us feel so atomised and lonely.

8

Justice

The evangelical church has been heavily involved with social justice. We have become interested in working to stop human trafficking, tackling the horror of debt and the establishment of food banks. There are campaigns and organisations that have thrived in these areas. It is a hugely encouraging development, although I am cautious about claiming that it is a rediscovery when many churches have been involved in such work for many decades. The nation is, and always has been, deeply indebted to the church and its social action.

But perhaps there has sometimes been a fear of concentrating on doing good in case it takes our eye off helping people on their way to salvation. I understand the fear that the social gospel might distract us from the saving gospel, and the fear is certainly not to be underestimated. There have been examples when this has happened. The trick, of course, is to do both.

But there is a deep dualism at work here and one that our Celtic ancestors may not have acknowledged. For them doing God and doing good were not mutually exclusive. This may have been because there were no social services to fall back on, no NHS and no care infrastructure – other than that offered by the monasteries anyway.

But the early Church – and I include the Celts in this – managed to hold together a striving for the alleviation of poverty and the like, along with the good news of Christ. They saw themselves as transformers of society as well as transformers of individuals. I think that the church takes that agenda on, too, today.

But I personally feel I need to speak more often in church about the challenge of justice and how God speaks up for the oppressed. The pay gap, racism, the class struggle, the piling up of wealth by the few are rarely discussed. We rarely question our own consumerism – do we need two cars or a holiday home? Is private education right? Should we give away some of our wealth? How many empty bedrooms do we have when other people are homeless?

Again, though, caution is needed. Jesus called us to take the plank from our own eye before criticising others. In any such thinking about justice I need to do some deep work on myself first.

The Celts can help us here. The kind of justice that transforms a society was at the centre of their way of doing things.

The great saints and scholars and social justice

The great theologian of the Celtic Christians, Pelagius, was a passionate advocate of social justice, and we have much to learn from our forebears' passion and where it came from. Above all, their quest for justice wasn't an add-on or a good-to-have. It sprang instead from their theology – their deep sense of the importance of the Incarnation. If God was one of us, then we must see all people as being of huge value to him.

If the human person is ultimately sacred, carrying the very image of God, then we must fight with all we have to be agents of transformation in the lives of those who are broken, homeless, hungry or whatever else.

Is doing good, doing to?

There is an intriguing nuance in the Celtic approach to social justice, and to understand it we need to start closer to home. Lilla Watson, academic, poet and campaigner, put it this way: 'If you have come here to help me, you are wasting your time. But if you have come because your liberation is bound up with mine, then let us work together.'[1]

This extraordinary statement tends to turn traditional notions of doing good on their head. Personally, I have become increasingly worried about working towards a social justice – doing good – that is essentially about simply doing good *to* others. In doing this we, the do-gooders, hold all the power. What if the striving for social justice was more mutual?

Lilla Watson hints at something very important. Simply turning up to fix things – people, communities – can be deeply patronising and result in cheap and shallow fixes. But if any act of setting people and communities free involves a mutual learning, flourishing and thriving, then that's different. The power relationship must be ended, and we who, for a season, serve others may one day be those who need sustaining ourselves. The act of justice is about mutual flourishing and is not an act but a way of life.

Much more than do-gooding

This idea would have rung a bell in Celtic times. For the Celts doing good was not just about altruism. Instead, it was a deep commitment to the Incarnation – that God is present in all equally and that in any caring exchange we are mutual beneficiaries. For the Celtic saints, social transformation went hand-in-hand with personal transformation.

We are called to be agents of deep change in society. Pelagius called for women to be taught to read (so they could study the Bible) and for the redistribution of wealth.[2] He argued against the presence of original sin in infants. St Patrick was insistent on the need for an end to slavery, partly because he had been a slave himself and knew the implications. In ridding Ireland of slavery, he changed the whole economic and social structure of the place. Social justice is at the heart of being a Christian. It could be argued that, had the Celtic Christians remained in a position of influence, slavery might not have needed ridding again by William Wilberforce.

What is our call today? What are our red lines? We need to be clear not just about what we are against, but what we are for. We are for human flourishing, we are for opportunity and we are for a society that values people and loves God. We can boldly proclaim that God wants us to transform our world and that we care about justice.

Behind the Celtic approach was theology. The theology spoke of the fact that each human being has ultimate worth and that we are enriched by contact with others and that we do good as a response to the essential goodness of God and his creation.

Pelagius wrote about our need to emulate Christ. Not just us personally, but also us as a Christian community. And that emulation meant paying attention to the outcast, the poor, the hungry and the sick. For Pelagius, the faith was lived out and witnessed by our acts. He was accused of denying grace in favour of acts, but nothing could be further from the truth. Instead, he emphasised that we have a role to play in bringing the kingdom and that actions speak as loudly as words.

It is tempting to see the Celtic tradition as essentially passive – taking joy in the world around, enjoying seclusion and the like. But one of the reasons that the Celtic Christians seemed such a threat to the

Roman Christian authorities was their radical edge when it came to action.

This desire to be out there, being like Christ and with an agenda to transform self, church and community, chimes well with us today. We see the injustice around us and we see where our communities are hurting.

The Celts give us free licence to keep on doing good and being transformed by those we work with and help. If we see our social outreach not as a separate action but part of the same impulse as worship, prayer and Bible study, then it no longer looks like social work and seems like being part of that great prayer that Jesus taught us – 'your kingdom come on earth as in heaven'.

So our Celtic forebears can help us as we think about the mission and vision of our churches. So many of us wonder whether the big problems that our society faces can be tackled at all. It seems as though we have mountains to climb. But perhaps the Celts also felt this way. Perhaps all generations do. But the trajectory of Celtic Christians included a deep commitment to the flourishing of society. It is encouraging to hear the passion for doing good echoing down the centuries. The modern church is part of this great historical quest.

This insight also helps us to see the Celtic way in the round and to see that it isn't just about having an experience of the holy. We too search for a faith that is all-encompassing and that helps us to make sense of the world we share with others. We stand with our brothers and sisters in yearning for justice and being part of its coming.

One charming example of the Celtic Christians' thirst for justice is the story of Bridgit of Kildare. It is likely that she was baptised by St Patrick and she certainly shared much in common with him.

Bridgit was the daughter of a king and she was certainly high maintenance. She liked to give her father's possessions away. One day, as her father was in a meeting with a prince aimed at offloading her on to him as his wife, Bridgit gave the king's most precious sword to a beggar. Finding out about the expensive habits of his prospective wife, the prince decided not to go ahead with the wedding. Bridgit decided to found a monastery. Giving possessions away seemed like second nature.

Bridgit asks of me a deep question: 'What can I give away?'

9

Saints Alive

Robyn Wrigley-Carr recently made an amazing discovery – the handwritten personal prayer books belonging to Evelyn Underhill. Underhill was a friend of C. S. Lewis (someone who had more than a hint of the Celtic Christian about himself) and an Anglo-Catholic. She was also the first woman to lead spiritual retreats in that tradition, and was a pacifist and a writer on spirituality. She has slipped from public prominence over the years and is now mainly a footnote.

Her little prayer asks the Lord that we might be changed by Jesus and the saints. It is beautiful and sets the ground for why we might take saints rather more seriously. It fairly sings off the page in its elegance and craft.

> Give us light, O Lord, that contemplating the love and patience of Jesus and His saints, we may be changed into love and patience. Take from us, by the contemplation of their example, all selfishness . . . Take from us all delicacy and fastidiousness. Take from us all cowardice and timidity. Take from us all self-love.[1]

For Underhill, getting to know and follow the example of the saints helps us to remove certain blockages on the spiritual path. By reading about them and thinking about their lives we might somehow ditch the baggage that we all carry – timidity, selfishness and, rather marvellously, fastidiousness. My goodness, is she on to something that we have been missing out on?

But her prayer has a second element. And this second element might be easy to pass over, although it is crucially important. The second element is a radical call to action – a call of hope:

Give us a share in their spirit of endurance. Give us a love of labour. Give us a love of the cross. Give us a love of hardships. Give us a spirit of courage. Give us a spirit of surrendered trust. That we may be willing to spend ourselves and be spent for the sake of Your children, in union with Your self-giving love.[2]

This moves from the minus part of the equation to the plusses. If we really inhabit the lives of the saints, we stand to gain something. That something is courage, hard work and trust.

Underhill was not a Celtic Christian, although she was deeply interested in Christian mysticism. But her prayer is like a rude awakening for many of us who may have put the saints in a box marked 'BEWARE'.

What's more, the Celtic saints have a particular character, timbre even. They are modest and local and their stories may be full of wonders but they have a sense of truthfulness about them.

The Celtic love of saints encourages us to think again and introduces a newness that helps us to understand our own lives. It is an odd thought that a Christian tradition from so long ago might speak into modern lives – but that's the beauty of it.

Glorious stories?

The stories of the Celtic saints are a distinct literature. There are some 85 accounts that we know
about and all of them were written many decades
after the actual lives of the saints concerned. Many
have the feel of an epic story with the saint cast as
superhero. The accounts coincided with a cult for
different saints, with pilgrimages taken to signifi-
cant places in their lives. In death the saints became
superstars and, it could be argued, formed part of a
strategy on behalf of the resurgent Catholic Church
to promote growth.

You might say that, with such a distance between
life and biography and with the somewhat stylised
content, we can comfortably ignore these historic
documents. But that would be to lose much. What's
more, there are very few contemporaneous documents for any aspect of ancient history.

Plus, when we read the accounts, they are stirring
documents and give us a window on to the way that
people thought – about the life of following Christ
and the power of being a follower. They also have an
intriguing ring of truth.

It is odd that during the lives of Celtic saints no one
saw fit to record their lives. Perhaps the Celts were

happy just to enjoy people's extraordinary lives and didn't feel the need to scribble about them. It is certainly true that the selection we now have available tends to concentrate on what have become the well-known saints.

There were thousands of Celtic saints. Places such as wells and towns were named after them and these names exist today, although shrouded in obscurity. The Celtic saints were local and approachable – they did not need to be canonised by the established Church. In this sense they seem more democratic than many of the power-saints we now have access to.

The saints felt as though they were part of the family and were comforting presences. One of the reasons I like the Celtic saints is that sense of closeness. I think that we, too, are in the presence of many local saints – our brothers and sisters in Christ who inspire us by their holiness, dedication and love for the Lord. Perhaps we could rediscover the Celtic way in recognising these saints.

Modern folk are looking for heroes and for good examples. We turn to sportspeople, rock stars and film stars and are disappointed when they have feet of clay. Many churches so emphasise the essential sinfulness and brokenness of people that we struggle to find anything good to say about a life. But we all respond well to good examples – just see the bookshops that are stuffed with biographies and autobiographies.

But if we time-travelled back to the days of the early Celtic Church we would have been familiar with local saintly people. We would have known the local well or glade that was named after them. We might talk about them and pray about them and perhaps sing songs about them. We would not have expected them to be perfect. The Celts mourned the presence of sin in the world and in ourselves. But we would perhaps have had more of a sense of gratitude to the examples around us and be more able to acknowledge them.

When you think about it, we are surrounded by humble saints today, as well.

I remember a person at one of my first churches. She was truly a saint. She knew everyone, visited the sick and was never one to criticise. Her patience was legendary and her humour brought us back to ourselves when we got too intense about everything. She would make a very good saint. Wouldn't it be good if she could become a saint by local consent, without us having to go through a lengthy canonisation process?

Saints and personal history

I came from a church that never mentioned saints, probably feeling that they were more appropriate in a Catholic setting. But the Celtic world is alive with the saints and we can be inspired by telling their stories. As I say, there are thousands of Celtic saints, often local holy people. Interestingly, when we get seekers coming to our Celtic services they are very interested in the life of our saint. They have no problem with the idea of saints, they don't find it a threat. They just enjoy the process of hearing his life story and taking away something that they can think about during the week.

We researched our saint and perhaps you too can find inspiring stories in him and the other Celtic saints.

The Celtic saints have much in their favour and chime with modern folk who are searching for practical examples of holiness. As Esther de Waal says in her book *The Celtic Way of Prayer*, 'Celtic saints are approachable, woven quite naturally into life just as would be any other member of an extended family.'[3]

As I researched the life of St Cuthbert, our saint here, I began to realise that snapshots from his life can be deeply relevant and inspiring. His life story, like those of so many of the saints, is genuinely enjoyable – with ups and downs, signs and wonders, meetings with angels and glorious encounters with wild animals who become friends. The popular TV show, *Snow Wolf Family and Me* with Gordon Buchanan, could almost be the story of a modern Celtic saint. In both, human beings encounter animals, not with mutual fear, but in an almost pre-Fall state of friendship and curiosity. To find out about our saint was great fun, but it was more than that. There were so many hooks and points of connection.

Celtic saints don't die by the sword; they are never austere and distant. One minute amazing things are happening to them, the next they are performing kind and gentle acts for local ordinary men and women. They feel like real people and their lack of violence or violent end somehow makes them rather wholesome. They like to feed the poor and they often have a touch of humour about them.

St Cuthbert

Our saint has inspired our service and we often tell his story.[4] This is how:

It is an early morning in March in the year 651. We are at the abbey in Melrose. It is just a short distance from Lindisfarne. Life in the kingdom is troubled. King Oswald had been killed just a few years before in battle. War is everywhere, and the country is in turmoil. It is not a settled place to be and people must have felt anxious a lot of the time.

The monastery is a place of welcome and safety. People come for education and sanctuary. The monks' lives are tough and marked by labour and prayer. This is no place of retreat from the world – it is at the heart of things. This week, though, is tougher than usual.

The great father abbot Boisil, known and loved by the brothers, has contracted plague and has only seven days to live. He has been a rock in this place – admired and relied upon. And it is hard when the father of the place is weakened.

Boisil knows he is dying but he still has time to make a difference and to shape the generation to come, especially a young man called Cuthbert, who is just 17. Cuthbert may be young but people have seen the divine spark in him. He is rough-and-ready, but how could he be truly ready for the next phase in his spiritual journey?

What can Boisil do in such a short time? He prays . . . tell me, Lord, how am I to guide this precious young man? He has an insight. He feels called to go to the Gospel of John and spend time with the boy studying it and letting it study them.

And so, this morning Boisil and Cuthbert are together. They can hear the birds outside. The swifts swooping in the air. They can feel the wind in the trees. The sounds of life in the monastery are all around. Despite the presence of an imminent death, life goes on. It always does. And perhaps in this deep sense of seasonality and continuance the brothers feel a sense of comfort.

Boisil explains that each day they will take a passage from St John and read it and then meditate on it. It is something concrete that they can do together. It will bring them together and allow Boisil to speak wisdom into the life of his young friend.

'I appointed you to go and bear fruit – fruit that will last . . . love one another . . .'

Young Cuthbert suddenly sees clearly. The verses strike home and open up new perceptions and a strong sense of God speaking. The Word has a way of opening us up – especially in times of trouble and anguish. This reading speaks deeply of the practical outworking of the faith in acts of kindness and love. The thing that is eternal is love – love never fails.

Another Bible verse comes to Cuthbert. It is from Paul's letter to the Galatians.

'For in Christ Jesus neither circumcision nor uncircumcision has any value. The only thing that counts is faith expressing itself through love.'[5]

Boisil begins speaking to young Cuthbert. They speak about the love of God. They explore how the Way is one of self-sacrifice. It is no easy journey and asks much of us. Boisil hopes that his pupil has understood it. That God's love is expressed not through staying within the walls of the holy place but in going out, spreading like the good vine. Love is the currency of the faith and it is something that we spread. We go out.

Each day they meet. The young novice and the loving brother are close by each other. They sit and pray and listen to the world in its activity and the sounds of nature and people. Each day the sun rises and sets. Each day there is the round of prayer. As each day passes, they become aware that Boisil is one day closer to meeting his maker – but then, so is Cuthbert, although the event seems a long way off.

Each day the eagle gospel soars in the young man's imagination. That gospel sums up this ancient Christianity. They drink deep of the faith and the Celtic way. Openness to women and their ministry. Wedding parties – feasting and celebration. The tender washing of the disciples' feet. The handing over of Jesus' mother to John to look after. Families are very important. Care for the old. These sessions begin to help Cuthbert see how the faith is worked out and lived and perhaps helps him to see something of his own approach.

And on the seventh day dear Boisil closes his Bible with a final 'Amen' and dies.

Years later, Cuthbert faces his own death. The church is in full revival. The poor have flocked to the faith. Cuthbert is back on Farne, alone. And he's sick, badly ill. Perhaps the plague has returned – the one he caught from his old friend Boisil. He is ill and weak and at a low ebb.

This is no picnic by the sea. This is a fight with the forces of temptation and evil. Cuthbert is dying and it is going to be a hard death. This will be no easy death in a warm bed, surrounded by a host of family. This is going to be a hard death, a brutal death – rather like the death our Lord suffered. Cuthbert is alone – and he feels abandoned and vulnerable. A storm is brewing. Hard deaths are perhaps the biggest trial. How to keep faith alive in such circumstances?

The island is in darkness, lashed. And Cuthbert's storm is exterior and interior too. He wrestles against his demons. Eventually, a friend gets to the island, a monk, and finds Cuthbert has dragged himself to a small hut by the shore. It is a pathetic sight.

This is not one of those interesting or quiet illnesses that people die from. Cuthbert has a vile sore that is weeping. It is disgusting and festering. He has moments when he feels God has abandoned him. Farne becomes Cuthbert's desert place, like Jesus' desert place. He is crucified with Jesus in some way. Is that not what awaits us all? None of us can be assured of a gentle end, can we?

But he keeps silent. Accepting what God has for him. Felgild the monk sits with him. Felgild becomes his successor on Lindisfarne. Felgild has a terrible facial disfigurement. Cuthbert prays for healing for his friend and his face is restored.

Cuthbert explains that Jesus alone can heal all that ails us. Another monk washes Cuthbert's sores and his feet. Cuthbert is peaceful, and says:

'This has been a great time of battling against the old enemy. I have fought the fight and finished the race.'

He dies. Jesus lives.

We have used this amazing account to help us to reflect on so many things. We have spoken about how we face trials and what a good death might look like. We have explored our personal desert places and movingly spoken to one another about those parts of our lives. In doing so, we have come to know one another better and to see the whole person rather than just the person who presents for church on Sunday.

We have talked about the sense of evil we sometimes feel. We have swapped stories of people who have influenced us and helped us on our journey. We have spoken about our love of nature and animals and how we have been brought closer to God by them. The saint's life has inspired us and we have wondered about how he kept going, despite all the setbacks he faced.

As we have lived the life of Cuthbert, we have begun to see amazing links between his life and our mission as a church. Cuthbert was the great localist. He spent much of his time reaching out to the local population. He ate with them and offered hospitality. He loved to teach and to meet the ordinary and poor folk. He was always out walking and eating with people. The locals loved him and took him to their heart.

We realised that if St Cuthbert were to visit us at our church – named after him – he would recognise much about our ministry of blessing. We hope that he would have been pleased with what he saw and that he would have seen something of his legacy in the way we do business around here.

In the past I would have simply seen the name of my church as an accident and got on with ministry. But now I think that in some way the spirit of our great saint lives on in this place.

We worship Jesus, but we also value his servant Cuthbert and we see no contradiction in this. Indeed, our acquaintance with our saint has enriched our spirituality and closeness to God and that can only be a very good thing.

10

Pilgrimage and Holy Places

We do tend to be quite static as Christians. Or is that not just Christians – as modern folk? That's not surprising at all. We live in a modern world that encourages us to put down roots. Many of us own or rent houses and are placed in a particular location. We have jobs that only give us, perhaps, one day off a week. Our children are at schools and have to be there each day of term time. We have a set time to work and an age at which we retire. We have insurance policies and pensions that need keeping up. We pay tax. Our churches work in our local communities. We tend to stay put. There is much that militates against us becoming wandering pilgrims, letting God lead us where he may. We cannot really live the life of a Celtic monk, even if that looks attractive. But we can learn from our forebears and we can wonder at the lives they lived.

Our model, or at least my model, has tended to be centred on church and a set day of the week – namely, Sunday. The week is all about the build-up to Sunday. The best that we tend to do in terms of pilgrimage is a visit to a Christian summer camp. We tend to stay put, partly because our churches have solid infrastructure that needs maintaining. For us modern folk, life is a lot more static in many ways.

Although we could add that we moderns do embark on secular pilgrimages all the time. We trek to football matches, shopping centres and theatres looking for an experience that is out of the ordinary.

But what would the Celts have to say about this?

We need to do some background digging. For the monks, travelling on pilgrimage was often part of their life. But so, too, was work in a monastery, praying and being alone. Manual work, contemplation and travel were all part of life – which seems like a balance we might learn from as well.

It has to be said that life was exceptionally hard for monks at the time. They would frequently submit to brutal penances and would starve themselves in acts of mortification of the flesh. We need to cast aside any rosy view of what life was like.

But what is true is that Celtic Christians as a whole did frequently travel and that they saw pilgrimage as part of their spiritual discipline and life. People were frequently on the way in the early days of the church. Indeed, the people of God were referred to as people of the way for centuries. This in itself points to a sense of movement in the early Church and a non-fixedness that goes along with a dynamic faith that saw itself as travelling always in God's world and their lives as a journey towards the truth.

When the gospel first came to Britain and Ireland under the Romans there were few roads. People tended to walk, and to walk on footpaths. It was natural to be on the move between villages and settlements. And walking changes the dynamics of any journey. On a walk, we notice more what is around us and we tend to take our time. On any walk, also, there will be a need to stop and rest, and in these rest periods we take stock and are grateful for stopping – and equally grateful when we start walking again.

The Celts were inveterate travellers not through simple wanderlust but because their reading of key Bible texts propelled them to travel lightly and be on the move often, and we have much to learn from them. They saw how Jesus was frequently on the move – as indeed was St Paul. The purposeful walk is part of the Way.

Plus, their definition of what made a place holy was so gloriously broad that it opened up many possibilities. Sometimes in our modern church we wonder what to make of holy places. We worry, perhaps, about taking our eyes off Jesus. But when we begin to appreciate that places can hold the spirit of God and the remembrance of prayers past, then we can enjoy more the sense of godly locations. This may, of course, sound a little far-fetched to some. But sometimes most of us have had a strong sense of God's presence in certain places. These 'thin places' where heaven and earth seem a bit closer are a real tonic to the weary traveller.

To be a pilgrim

Films such as Emilio Estevez' 2010 epic *The Way*[1] perhaps point to a very modern image and understanding of pilgrimage. *The Way* stars Estevez' father, Michael Sheen. Sheen plays Tom, the American doctor who goes to France following the death of his adult son, killed in the Pyrenees during a storm while walking the Camino de Santiago, also known as the Way of St James.

As a homage to his estranged and wayward son, the father completes the son's Camino and meets others from around the world (three in particular), all broken and looking for greater meaning in their lives.

It is a touching film, but perhaps it is most interesting in that it encapsulates our mixed and incomplete understanding of pilgrimages. Are they opportunities for a holy moment for spiritual development and meeting God at a specific time and place? In one sense the film makes consumerism the hero of the piece. The broken pilgrims are all searching for breakthrough and release from different blocks in the road, but we are never quite clear what it is that they seek or find. Should we all down tools and trek over to Spain for a dose of pilgrimage?

The Celtic Christians had a far more complete understanding of both pilgrimage and seclusion – we often call this a retreat.

So what could we learn from the Celtic Christians' attitude to pilgrimage?

For a start, they had a deep sense that **the journey was as important as the destination**. This was probably because the journey took time and couldn't be hurried.

So many of the prayers we have handed down to us from the Celtic tradition are about journeys. I certainly would like to value the getting there as much as the 'there' itself. There were no motorcars for the Celtic Christians – they mainly walked and so they appreciated the journey. We can imagine them savouring the sights and sounds and the earth and grass beneath their feet. We have such an ability to plan and to anticipate our destination. The internet has revolutionised travel. We can see everything about our destination before we get there and we can plan the journey in minute detail.

But what if we and a group of friends crafted a small boat and set off with sail but no oars and just let God get us to wherever he chose? This kind of pilgrimage journey was not uncommon, even if it sounds highly dangerous, even reckless, to us. In an age when we always know where we are and are going, via satnav and the like, the ability to simply set off and trust the rules of being on the pilgrimage trail sounds wildly liberating. But those who undertook such heroic journeys knew that they were dangerous, and their lives were in peril.

The name for those who just wandered was 'wandering saints' and they simply set out with no destination in mind, letting themselves be led by the Holy Spirit. Where they finally came to a halt became known as the place of their resurrection.

They saw the aim of pilgrimage as leading to some kind of **personal resurrection** and so they anticipated that not all the journey would be easy and the destination might not be perfect.

The Celtic Christians, as Ian Bradley points out in *The Celtic Way*, saw pilgrimage as a metaphorical living out of deep personal change – a journey towards God through repentance, resurrection and rebirth. This, of course, is far more than Christian sightseeing or tourism. It is a call to take pilgrimage seriously. It was the very opposite of escapism because it asks something of us, not least the ability to trust God and be honest with him.

Pilgrimages were not just about holy moments; they were also a missionary activity that involved the opportunity to get close to people and share time with them and explain the hope the pilgrims had in the gospel.

So what might your common-or-garden pastor make of such things? Setting sail on a home-made boat and ending up on the shores of America seems well beyond us these days. But despite this we are inspired, as the Celtic Christians were, by the story of an aged St Brendan doing just this and becoming the patron saint of adventurers.

We shy away from difficult desert places and might be scared of them as places of internal resurrection. We plan until the cows come home and it makes us feel safe – although the chaos of the world tends to overcome even the best-laid plans.

But there is something here for us perhaps. Do we need to think about pilgrimages again, even if we don't do them exactly as they used to?

Evangelicals and the modern pilgrimage

Is it possible to become people of pilgrimage again? This might mean being less attached to our buildings and more prepared to get out there into the world. It feels a bit risky.

So could we allow ourselves to get lost with God? Could we stop making lists and being purposeful in everything and simply either be or do something frivolous? (Jesus was after all three days late for a death, so he could get distracted.)

If the all-out trip to the US without oars is beyond us, just some unplanned time where we can journey a while without a destination in sight can be tremendously liberating. This is the case even if it only helps us to stop fretting about the day-to-day debris of our lives and take ourselves a little less seriously. It is also a good focus to see our lives not as a random series of events but as a journey we make with others towards faith.

Some say that the Celtic tradition described the Holy Spirit as the wild goose – a bird that was unpredictable and untamed, and this encourages us to break some of the chains of our routines. The world won't stop if we ditch our phones and have time to be a pilgrim again.

Can we as a church actually plan a pilgrimage – perhaps to something associated with whatever saint our church is associated with? It isn't making an idol of that saint or downplaying Jesus. Instead, it is about adding extra texture to our spiritual journey.

What we can perhaps learn from our Celtic forebears is something of the pilgrim mindset. In our regimented lives, this can act as a catalyst for simply enjoying the moment and celebrating God's closeness. The secular business of mindfulness has its roots in the pilgrim mindset. Stopping to be present and open to wandering and finding out is like taking a stroll while on holiday and seeing what we find, instead of being chained to the dictates of the guidebook.

11

Our Celtic Service

There are as many different ways to put together a Celtic service as there are services. There are rich resources from the Iona and Northumbria Communities and we have drawn heavily from them. The internet has a depth and variety of poems and liturgies and the shops have many excellent books on Celtic Christianity. Celtic Christianity may not yet be mainstream, but there is some very thoughtful and authentic stuff out there. This is perhaps where to start any adventure with the Celts.

Our aim was to create an oasis of calm and a place where we could hear from the Celtic Christians. We wanted a space and time where we might be happy to pause – rather like the pause on a pilgrimage walk. We wanted something that did not seem hurried and where the words – liturgies, poems and readings – were allowed to speak and not be mediated through the priest or through imposed interpretation.

This is quite a challenge for me. We tend to filter the Word through preachers. We tend to pray extempore through those who specialise in prayer. We wanted to step back and allow the past to speak to us – not because it was closer to God, but because it would strike a different note that would allow us to come closer to God.

Our Celtic service was not a replacement for what we had – we wanted an addition that would sit alongside our vibrant and creative modern services. In this I think there is something quite innovative. It is a challenge to step outside any tradition. The charismatic tradition which I hold in high esteem would characterise itself as one that was free and without rules. But introducing a Celtic service might challenge that kind of statement. Sometimes we are free, but only free to do what we have always been doing.

It helped that I'd been using Celtic blessings at services for a while and that I'd been doing readings from Celtic books and resources during times of reflection in church. Each time I did this people would come and ask if we could have more of this. They said that it made them feel peaceful and somehow gave a perspective on God that they had missed. We had planted a seed and that was what we were building on.

One season over the Lent period I read from one of David Adam's books. The response was surprising. People were very clearly taking everything in, and after each reading people would come up and ask me about it. I realised that we had a need for this, and it was deeply affecting the listeners. This was good because I loved the things I was reading as well. It was what I was reading back at the vicarage for my own spiritual food.

It wasn't that the usual services we ran were wrong or that we wanted to replace them. But the common perception here was that sometimes we felt tired, and sometimes we needed a time to step back, be quiet and listen to ancient words that would encourage us. The congregation had a yearning for something that was more contemplative. They loved the excitement and drive of our morning service, or the liturgical Communion service, but there was room for something new.

We detected that many of the people who came to church, or we bumped into in our daily lives, weren't particularly 'Christian' but that they did have an awe and wonder at the world of nature and that they loved to listen to poetry and then be swept up into what Eugene Peterson calls 'the unforced rhythms of grace'.[1]

Many of the people we met had visited 'holy' places such as Lindisfarne. Others enjoyed watching programmes about this kind of place. Most seemed restless and felt anxious or wanting the assurance that God protects or that families matter or that we are in safe hands. London is a fast-paced city and we underestimate how much it takes out of us. We get tired and a bit frazzled and we always seem to be in a rush. Is there scope to go a bit slower and to simply enjoy God's company for a while?

After so much encouragement we decided to put together our first Celtic service and see how it worked out. We wanted it to be easy to run – so we had no live music or singing and no specially written sermon. Our aim was that it should feel natural and have the same shape and rhythm each time.

We wanted to listen to music – the kind of listening that didn't require us to sing. In a way, this was so we could be receivers – we could simply allow ourselves to be swept away and let God do the work. Our aim was to soak into the music and let ourselves be rested.

We were blessed with a lady chapel that hadn't been used for years, and a lovely little space it was. People commented on how it felt 'holy', although they weren't quite sure what that meant. What it said to us was that they had a sense of place – and that is quite a Celtic way of looking at the world. Our little chapel was the ideal place for us to set up our service.

Perhaps more interesting is the way we have put together building blocks, how we have publicised our service and how it has developed. We started simply and we have continued simply and it's that radical simplicity that is part of the charm of our Celtic service.

It is easy to come to and easy to lead and we can put all our energy into simply being present and listening to the wisdom of our forebears. It feels peaceful and that is a rare commodity indeed.

The building blocks

We wanted our service to be very different from our normal services. Any church space has the capacity to be adapted and for certain aspects to be picked out for worship. In some ways this was very healthy because it helped us to take a close look at what we had available and to wonder how we might use and adapt it. We sometimes get trapped into using our space the same way each week, but by thinking about a new kind of service we can liberate a fresh sacred environment.

We weren't competing or overlapping with what we already had and we anticipated that for many this might be the only service they came to. This was a break from our traditions, but we were very comfortable with that. It was an odd reversal of what normally happens. We weren't ditching the traditional service and adding an informal one. We were adding something more formal to our existing mix.

This is what we do.

We dress our chapel with candles both on the altar and on the window ledges. The candles are a signal of quiet and of our supplications to God. We group them on the altar and light them, so when people come the church is aglow. They look very beautiful and establish a sense of what is about to come.

We turn the lighting down and strip the altar back to a simple white cotton cloth. The stripped-back quality makes a statement. As in many evangelical churches, our morning service is a big production number. We have microphones and a screen and projector and a band. It is exciting and we take a lot of time to put it together each week. We show videos and we have interaction. There are refreshments and a children's church. Each service is devised anew and there is a thirst for variety. I sometimes say that it has many moving parts.

Our Celtic service is as simple as it is possible to be with just a simple service sheet. We keep the same service each time. The altar has no adornments other than some candles.

The aim is to do nothing that will distract from the words and music. Before people come, we make sure the place is warm and we put on some music – usually something thoughtful, choral and with a monastic flavour. We don't choose well-known hymns as we feel people might be tempted to sing – we want them to reflect and simply to be still.

As people arrive, we encourage them to sit quietly for a while, to listen and be still. We are happy for this stillness to last some time, so that latecomers can be seated and ready. Silence is as much a part of this service as are words. In the silence we can begin to relax and let God work on us. Sometimes we need to practise letting our anxious thoughts and distractions subside. Silence is a gift. It is especially a gift in a city and in a place crowded with people and activity. This gift of silence seems to us to be one of the ways that a Celtic service can add further depth to what we do.

Our Celtic forebears frequently held their services outside. They would have heard the wind and the birds – harmonious sounds. They would have had access to silence, and we claim access to it in our service.

We spend some time being thankful. We might use an old prayer like this:

All thanks and praise and worship be unto thee, O God, for all that thou hast given unto us, and as thou hast given the life of our body to win the food of this world, so grant us the life eternal to show forth thy glory.[2]

Many of us modern folk rarely find time to be thankful for what we've got and been given. Although maybe that's a phenomenon that's as old as the hills – after all, Jesus tells the tale of healing a whole bunch of people with leprosy and only one coming back to say thank you.

The little West Highlanders' prayer above does the act of saying thanks with such panache that it is most winning. Like so many of the prayers of the

Celtic Christians, it uses the most poetic and attractive of images. Here's another we may use:

> O God of the elements, glory be unto thee. Grant us thine own hand on our rudder-helm and thy love behind on the great heaving waters . . .[3]

We get a picture of the God of might – ruler of the elements – and then we give thanks for the help we have in staying safe on the 'sea', that Christ is steering the boat of our lives, his hand firmly on the rudder and the waters stilled by his abiding love.

Poem-prayers like these, delivered with striking clarity, creativity and economy, help us to open up more generally and to be thankful for all our many blessings. Being blessed and feeling blessed is no pagan impulse – the wishing for an amulet to protect us. Instead, it speaks into the deepest recesses of our being. Even in the midst of trouble we sometimes get a moment of crystalline insight that we are still blessed in so many ways. The desire to hear a blessing bestowed upon us is part of the safety blanket that we all need – however strong we are.

David Adam, in his introduction to G. R. D. McLean's *Prayers of the Western Highlanders*, explains how prayers such as those above taught him a new way of praying. More than that, they were a revelation: 'I was immediately attracted by the rhythm and earthiness of the prayers, which offered a less formalized and more natural way of conversing with God.'

Simple yet beautiful prayer-poems like these seem to be revelatory for many of the guests at our Celtic service. Many tell us that they had no idea such prayers and such an approach to prayer existed, and that it was something they had been searching for. In our modern church we concentrate often on so many things, but the simple act of receiving a blessing can seem from another time and tradition. But at our service the act of creative and beautifully poetic blessing is just that. And when we feel blessed then it is natural to want to be thankful.

In the case of thanksgiving, many non-Christians tell us that it is a relief to have someone to actually say thank you to – God.

We then follow with either a Communion or a Compline service, using words from the resources available. Our simple service sheet fits on to an A4 sheet folded over. We tend to keep the same service each time, as people have enjoyed becoming familiar with it.

We encourage people when they are seated to be comfortable and to clear their minds and be as peaceful as they can. Sometimes they close their eyes for a while or just sit and make themselves comfortable.

In each service we take breaks for readings. These will usually be from a Celtic book of some kind. They can be prayers or lives of the saints or readings from books with a contemplative edge. We don't have a sermon, but we do have a Bible reading. The readings are delivered slowly, with time to think after each reading. Sometimes we might read a poem. At other times we might read a tale of yesteryear or something from St Cuthbert's life. After each reading we pause and let it sink in. We wait on the presence of the Lord.

At points throughout the service we stop to reflect and be still and listen to music. People visibly relax as we play the music and they often feel a great sense of lightness.

We always end with a blessing. There are so many Celtic blessings but the following is a favourite. We use it at our service and at many of our other services too.

> May the road rise up to meet you.
> May the wind be always at your back.
> May the sun shine warm upon your face;
> the rains fall soft upon your fields and until we meet again,
> may God hold you in the palm of His hand.[4]

It may be familiar to many, but it wasn't familiar to us. We had never come across it before, although many of our Roman Catholic friends were very familiar with it.

People tell me that it gives them a sense of freedom and that they love the sense of the natural world breaking through and the strange sense of pilgrimage it encapsulates. They love that it holds forth the prospect that we will be meeting again and that we are all on the journey together in some way.

The use of Celtic prayers with their themes of community and care for the earth are valuable reminders for us evangelicals – and help us steer away from an atomised faith that seems only interested in high-octane holy moments and personal salvation. It is also something of a relief to be able to rely on ancient prayers that have stood the test of time and to realise that we do not need to dredge up our own impromptu prayers when we don't feel like doing it.

The overall effect, though, is to let the words and music speak and to have time to be still and to reflect. We often include a prayer for protection and a poem or prayer from a Celtic resource about God being near and the beauty of nature and God's baptising of the world.

People tell us that they love this service and that they would not miss it for the world.

Publicity

We produced posters and flyers featuring a Celtic cross and put these on our street-side noticeboard. We used word-of-mouth and we put a small article about our service in our estate magazine.

We realised that people would come as we began to receive calls about the service in advance and people popped in to find out what it was about. We got interest from unexpected quarters and many of our neighbours from different faiths wanted to know more.

We continue to send out leaflets and tell people about our service. It is on our church website as well and word-of-mouth is also a powerful tool.

How it has developed

We have seen steady growth and many come from the local area who attend no other service at all. We have a core of people in their 20s and 30s, some who are not believers and some who are. They tell us that this feels like church and that they feel peaceful and calm after the service.

We notice that many seekers actually like a church that feels a bit churchy. They enjoy a sense of the ancient rhythms and an experience that is both rather exotic and strangely comforting.

We have people who have been searching for a Sunday evening service as most other local ones have closed. We take no collection, seeing this service as a simple blessing. Not taking a collection is rather an interesting experience. In fact, people very much appreciate it. This is not because they are unwilling to part with money. It is just that they associate church with always being asked for money. Not being asked for a donation seems like a beautiful free gift from us and from God. Taking money out of the equation is liberating.

Our chapel is full to capacity and we are moving from holding the service once a month to holding it every Sunday evening at six o'clock. We chose this time so that people could come and then get home for their tea. They go back and look forward to their Sunday evening. They tell us that they feel comforted. The comfort of the service mixed with a cup of hot milk and a Sunday evening with the TV is like wrapping a warm blanket around you.

There are certain themes we come back to time and again. God is close. God baptised the world and all that is in it. God protects and saves. We make sure that we always read the Gospel. The themes are one of the things that give the service a sense of continuity. We don't look for novel themes or readings.

The Celtic service as our evangelical heritage

It may be that our service raises as many questions as it answers. Is it just a piece of opportunism that will run out of steam? How on earth does this kind of service fit in with a very evangelical church with charismatic leanings? Does the service have any real depth?

These are good questions and we will need to unpick them over the years. But what I can say is that the Celtic service has fitted surprisingly well with us as an evangelical church – it doesn't feel like a fudge and it feels natural. Now that is, of course, a subjective judgement – but so much of church life is. Church is an art not a science. Ready formulas are unlikely to work, and what works well in one place may not work well in another.

But, yes, it fills some gaps which we felt were missing from our spiritual platter and from many evangelical churches. We were short on silence on a Sunday and we were short on poetry. That's fine, as our biggest service wasn't really the place for these. There was a yearning for a service that felt organic.

But we did find some real points of connection.

Our Celtic service tends to focus on themes that we have picked up on for years within our evangelical tradition – the presence of evil, the feeling of needing protection and the love of creation. By articulating these in the evening, we reinforced things we'd spoken about over the years. So the service doesn't feel like an alien takeover or a set of unorthodox premises that sit uncomfortably with our traditions. Instead, it feels a bit like coming home, taking its place among all that is good about our majority tradition.

As an evangelical I generally want to get back to basics – to strip away all that gets in the way of our journey with God. The Celtic service seemed to allow us to do this, although not in a way we had expected. Its simplicity is a bonus and that idea of doing something simple was something we had long believed in.

There is another way that this service, and the ancient prayers we utter in it, really help us. In praying the simple everyday prayers of Celtic Christians, we began to have a richer understanding both of prayer and of what holy moments actually are. We have had a flourishing of our understanding of the presence of the Holy Spirit. Or put another way, we have opened up our understanding and perception of the holy in the everyday.

We realised that prayers written and said by others, even by others over the centuries, were as packed with the Holy Spirit as the most fervent impromptu prayers. Indeed, the fact that we did not have to make up prayers on the spot liberated everyone to inhabit the ancient prayers for themselves. The treasury of ancient prayers and poems helped us deeply. It wasn't a case of either/or, it was that both paths had spiritual potential, and sometimes, on a wet Sunday evening, praying the prayers of the ancient Hebridean community, with their homeliness and sense of community and joy, could help us build both into our lives as well.

We felt a kinship with the ancient writings because they have a surprisingly modern way of looking at life. We began to inhabit the prayers and claim them as our own.

The service and the prayers released a yearning and a great love of creation. It was as though we saw the faith afresh and felt we were coming home.

Tokenism

I think I can hear the complaint that what we are doing is tokenism. It was something that I worried about and that at least one of my colleagues in ministry felt that we were doing.

Perhaps we are play-acting being Celtic Christians, only to move on with this having no impact on our faith life or journey towards God as a church. This voice needs to be heard. In one way whether it is or isn't tokenism is neither here nor there. Personally, I am the ultimate pragmatist. St Paul himself showed a level of spiritual practice pragmatism. He was prepared to walk inside the spiritual shoes of other ethnicities and spiritualities in order to win people for the Lord.

Another way of saying the same thing in a more positive way is to assert that we are flexible, pliable – able to gather the best from a variety of traditions. Being too fixed in a world that is able to move quickly is not always a virtue. We can be left standing while everyone else has moved on.

But there is a profound way in which our Celtic service and the spirituality that lies throughout it has reinforced us and propelled us forward. It has dovetailed perfectly with our great mission which we cast as 'to be a blessing'.

Perhaps the most influential part of our Celtic service has been the blessings we have used. For the Celts, blessing was a way of life – which may explain why they have so many beautiful ones. If we come from a God of infinite goodness and we all bear his imprint then accepting his blessing and blessing him in return is the way of the world.

What if we lived our lives in the knowledge of God's blessing? Our response, as it was for our Celtic brothers and sisters, was the impulse to be a blessing to others – to our friends and families, to our communities and to the world. Living with blessing makes us more compassionate and generous, and where else do we find this in our atomised world?

We sometimes use the following blessing to end our service. It helps people to feel safe and asserts that God is not just in charge, but that he wants to bless us and for us to be people who carry that blessing with us. The Celtic Christians put much store on blessings. They had blessings for everything – for the morning, evening and even for milking the cows. They blessed the simple business of waking up in the morning and finding oneself still breathing. It was a way of life that celebrated being blessed and worked to pass it on. Always the blessing was in the name of the Trinity.

God's blessing be yours,
And well may it befall you;
Christ's blessing be yours,
And well be you entreated;
Spirit's blessing be yours,
And well spend you your lives,
Each day that you rise up,
Each day that you lie down.[5]

This blessing of the Trinity speaks deeply to us. It speaks deeply to seekers who come to our service. If we do not believe in God, who is there to bless us? Who has the authority to do it and how can we feel that we are blessed?

But the Celtic way is no simple feel-good factor. There is a deep impulse to mission behind this apparently simple act. Sometimes our evangelical churches can make us feel that we are weighed down by sin – although of course saved by grace. But the Celtic way seems to speak of a deep blessedness – that God is happy with us. That doesn't mean that the blessing is about health and wealth – not at all. The Celts were aware of our deep need for repentance, but they were not prisoners to guilt.

Yes, we are told to take up our cross and follow Jesus. Suffering is a given, and the Celts knew this profoundly. They understood the corrosion of sin as well. They were not happy optimists, unaware of all that is wrong and all that ails us. But if at the heart of the world is a good creation, an incarnational God and a spirit of deep and abiding blessedness, then it encourages us to be thankful for the fact that we are alive and that God is in the image of everyone and everything we come across.

This single insight chimed very well with us. My earliest experience of attending a charismatic church, when I was not a Christian, was the beautiful and profound joy I saw on the faces of the believers. I loved that this church was not weighed down by gloom and that it celebrated what was good. I looked at those around me and sincerely wanted to be more like them. The sense of blessedness that our Celtic forebears hand on to us in the modern church is actually very familiar, especially to those of us who went to a church that had a smile on its face.

When we finish one of our Celtic services with a blessing, we go out into the night with a new sense of peace and purpose. We use the ancient words because they have stood the test of time. And in their homely imagery and application to day-to-day lives we feel a bit better than when we came into church. It seems to us that feeling better when one leaves church than when one arrived is something of a given.

We do not do this as a substitute for other aspects of our spirituality. We have it as something new and extra and it feels natural to us. We take the blessing into our families and into our jobs and day-to-day activities. Yes, it is administered by the priest, but we all receive it, including the minister.

12

Final Word: Jesus, Our Church and the Celtic Tradition

Perhaps you have a question about where Jesus is in all this? Perhaps you have a worry that it sounds nice, but is too undemanding. Perhaps you worry that we have lost Jesus along the way in a fluffy celebration of nature and its creatures. It is certainly worth checking. It is always easier to talk about Christian history or ethics than to spend time with Jesus. We need to guard about talking about the faith rather than living it.

Jesus and the Celts

The Celts may have been Trinitarian but they never lost sight of Jesus and we don't either. They had a number of pictures of him – a number of insights. Christ can be looked upon in different ways, and different aspects and interpretations of his character and mission give us different images – all of course, though, the same God. The pungency and variety of the images for Christ and the understanding of him are rather wonderful.

For them, he was the King of the Elements, the Son of the Light. For those of us who are uncomfortable with some of the 'boyfriend' imagery of Christ that we are served up, the Celtic image is good and strong. Take the following, for instance:

Shepherd of the field
Jesus thou our shield
Master, Lord of angel host,
Feed us, lead us coast to coast
Jesus weald to weald
By the lamb-blood sealed.[1]

This was just one of the striking images that they used – each relevant to us today. Jesus the shepherd we understand, although we may not be shepherds ourselves. A shepherd needs sheep that follow him and him alone – and for us moderns the sheep image is a little difficult. But the moment we see ourselves as sheep, we are liberated from our own perfection-ism, self-love and over-control. Christ is a working shepherd – the shepherd out in the field in rain or shine. He is the shepherd who would die for the sin-gle stray and naughty sheep, the sheep who insists on running off. Now a sheep like that is one most of us can identify with.

But the picture is as intertwined and intricate as a great Celtic knot. Jesus is our shield and leader of the great angelic forces – a kind of battle commander ready to fight on our behalf. And with that pedigree, who could doubt that he can feed and lead us too? Christ is the ultimate victor. He is the shield we can hide behind and be protected by. And when in our lives we seem hard-pressed from every side, then the shield image is one we can cling to and own a little as well.

Of course, he is also the Lamb of God, and that beautiful image sits interestingly beside the battle images. It is the essential paradox of the incarnate God – both God and man.

God is commander of the angels. We sometimes give little thought to this picture of Christ – espe-cially if our theology is not very strong on angels. But remember, Jesus not only believed in angels, he also needed their help in order to get to the Cross. The angels sustained him and uttered words that built his courage. And in this image Christ is now the leader of the angelic army – ready to do battle in the heavenly realms. It is a thoroughly awesome image in its truest sense. The Christ ready for battle with legions of mighty supernatural beings at his right hand. It is an image as far removed from the Jesus-our-mate language as can be imagined.

And this Christ calls us through the words of the ancient poem. Of course, in other Celtic poems we get a picture of Christ the child at his mother's breast or the companion making himself at home in our kitchen.

We need a range of metaphors and images to help us to grasp Christ. After all, our language will always be insufficient when trying to describe and thank the maker of the universe. One option is to descend into silence in the face of such immensity. Another is to use the language we have to picture God in ways that bring out aspects of him.

In just a few lines here we have a rich banquet of imagery. There is also a cry that this very God might lead us in our humble everyday path. The cosmic and the everyday nestle comfortably in the ancient words and outlook. Perhaps there was less to get in the way of Christ in a less complex and less selfish and self-obsessed world.

The Celts were super-evangelists, not semi-pagan tree-huggers. They wanted others to become Christians. They wanted the faith to grow, and it did. They wanted people to know our Lord and to become disciples. So we must put away any thoughts that they were just simple spiritual seekers. They loved Christ and were in awe of him, but they never let fear of his might put them off from approaching him.

This realisation clears away one of the main objections that some in the modern church have to the Celtic way.

St Cuthbert was known as the *Fire of the North,* so quickly did the gospel of Christ spread. For all their homely and comforting ways, the Celts were Christians of passion and commitment. Their saints were accompanied by signs and wonders, healings and visions. The faith crackled to life and spread swiftly. As a bishop, Cuthbert would travel to the wild and isolated hamlets and settlements. He would sit and eat with common people – thought by many to be beyond the reach of the gospel. He travelled always on foot, often with a young novice for company. He ditched the bishop's ceremonial horse.

He would explain his hope and trust in Jesus and many were converted. His ministry was as far from pantheism as one could imagine. There was an urgency that people needed to be saved – and that chimes totally with what we evangelicals believe.

Jesus is the Lord of nature, and the Celts, in their prayers and songs and poems, acknowledge and celebrate this. For them Jesus was close – a protector and friend. Again, this is a concept that we welcome and that many of us live out day to day.

We have found that our exposure to Celtic spirituality as a church has been nothing but positive. We have reconnected with a long-forgotten sense of wonder in the world around us. The poems and prayers from the rugged parts of the country have connected with our own love of the rugged places. Even though we are all city-dwellers, we have a deep love and communal appreciation for the world we live in and the creatures we share it with. Indeed, the green agenda of the Celts is something, as an evangelical church, we have tended to ignore.

The green agenda is ever growing and the love needed for our beautiful planet is now a matter of great urgency. It is a relief to know that there is a tradition that already has this at its heart and that we can borrow from.

As a church with charismatic leanings, we have long held to the God who is close through the working of the Holy Spirit. We pray for healings. We expect to see signs of God's presence. The Celtic way simply reinforces this – the Celts were aware of God in everything and in the everyday and frequently experienced visions and dreams from him. Again, this simply dovetails with our own spirituality – but it gives us new poems, prayers and practices.

Over the years we have embraced creativity in worship – with plays and songs and banners. A full-on service at one of the large charismatic churches takes a great deal of love and creativity. The creativity of the Celts – with Jesus the great creator at the helm – chimes. Creativity is good because God is the most creative being and blesses such activity. Being with Jesus was never stale, or run-of-the-mill. He was a creative teacher. He used startling images and spoke thought-provoking parables. He worked miracles. And so the creativity of the Celtic way with language is a joy rather than a threat.

But again, we have added new resources and insights. So the Celtic journey has been less strange than we imagined, and we have not lost sight of Jesus. Instead it has seemed like a long-lost friend joining us.

But we have been exposed to new things, and these have been welcome. Our service without a sermon, with time to listen and think and with the words of deep and ancient faith, has unearthed the riches of silence and contemplation. Our use of candles and icons and symbols has felt right and proper and not mumbo-jumbo. And the blessings and prayers for protection have opened our eyes to the spiritual battles around us and reassured us that the Trinity and the angels are on the case. We are reverent towards the materials that we have, and we spend time praying about what we are doing.

We are not fully signed up Celtic Christians. But our exposure to this spirituality has been wonderful and we do commend it.

There has been a very chequered past between evangelicals and the Celtic Church. The Celts' optimistic belief in the essential goodness of creation and that God is within all creatures drew sharp criticism from those with a view of the Cross that stressed substitutionary atonement and used the language of the law courts. Scottish Calvinism tried hard to wipe Celtic spirituality from the map and nearly succeeded.

Time to make up

My feeling is that it is time to make up, make good and see all that is good in this ancient expression of the faith. The Celts were not simple wide-eyed nature lovers. They were not pagans disguised as Christians. Their spirituality understood the depths of depravity and evil caused by sin and the dangers of the devil and his evil minions. It is robust enough to see life in full. They knew that Jesus is our protector and Lord. As the ancient Celtic prayer for protection goes:

> I am placing my soul and my body
> Under thy guarding this night, O Christ,
> O thou Son of the tears, of the wounds of the piercings,
> May thy cross this night be shielding me.[2]

I am sure we can all say 'Amen' to that. And as we do, another of the great Celtic pictures comes to mind. This time it is of us, our souls and bodies, placed under the great guard of Jesus. He stands watch as we sleep. He does not grow weary – keeping us safe from the slings and arrows of the devil.

We make the decision to trust him and he undertakes to be our guard and our defender. But what kind of guardian do we have? – what kind of superhero? If we can have a range of images then we can more easily visualise and inhabit who God is – even though he is cloaked in mystery and awe.

He is, the prayer-poem tells us, the Son of tears with his wounds still fresh – as always. Christ suffered, and his suffering was a way of answering Job's great riposte to God the Father – 'You do not know what it is like to be a person.' The Celtic Christians understood Christ's suffering and did not make light of it. In this understanding of suffering, we can look suffering in the face ourselves. The Celtic way helps us to ally ourselves with the suffering of God and to see that suffering is not a punishment, but rather a part of life.

And it is not just Jesus that casts a protective shadow over us, it is his precious Cross. The Cross stands as a barrier to all that would disturb us, assail us, get at us. We venerate the Cross and see it as the defining moment of history. We preach about it and know its importance.

Our forebears knew the power of the Cross too. They lived in its shadow and understood its might. It is incredibly comforting, after a tough day, when the world seems hostile and grim, to be offered the chance to be loved and protected. However old we are, we never quite lose our fear of the dark. We never lose that vulnerability when we sleep – unconscious and helpless. In Christ's darkest hour his followers could not keep awake. We are all guilty of sleeping on the spiritual job. But Christ will not sleep as he prepares to guard us and we can sleep in peace and take our rest.

Further Reading

Adam, David, *The Edge of Glory*, SPCK, 1985.

Adam, David, *Fire of the North: The Life of St Cuthbert*, SPCK, 2008.

Allchin, A. M., *Praise Above All: Discovering the Welsh Tradition*, University of Wales Press, 1991.

Bradley, Ian, *The Celtic Way*, Darton, Longman & Todd, 2003 (2nd edition).

Brueggemann, Walter, *A Gospel of Hope*, Hodder & Stoughton, 2018.

Brueggemann, Walter, *The Prophetic Imagination*, Fortress Press, 2018 (40th Anniversary edition).

Carmichael, Alexander, *Carmina Gadelica: Hymns and Incantations*, Floris Books, 2006.

De Waal, Esther, *The Celtic Way of Prayer*, Doubleday, 1997.

Earle, Mary C., *Celtic Christian Spirituality*, SPCK, 2012.

Maclean, Alistair. *Hebridean Altars: The Spirit of an Island Race*, Wipf & Stock, 2013, wipfandstock.com

McIntosh, Kenneth, *Celtic Nature Prayers*, Anamchara Books, 2015.

McIntosh, Kenneth, *Water from an Ancient Well*, Anamchara Books, 2011.

McLean, G. R. D., *Prayers of the Western Highlanders*, SPCK, 2008.

Miller, Calvin, *The Path of Celtic Prayer*, The Bible Reading Fellowship, 2008.

Mitton, Michael, *Restoring the Woven Cord*, The Bible Reading Fellowship, 2019 edition.

Mitton, Michael, *Travellers of the Heart*, The Bible Reading Fellowship, 2013.

Newell, J. Philip, *Listening for the Heartbeat of God*, SPCK, 1997.

O'Loughlin, Thomas, *Journeys on the Edges*, Darton, Longman & Todd, 2000.

Simpson, Ray, *A Holy Island Prayer Book*, Canterbury Press, 2002.

Simpson, Ray, *Exploring Celtic Spirituality*, Kevin Mayhew, 2004.

Underhill, Evelyn, *Evelyn Underhill's Prayer Book*, SPCK, 2018.

Notes

[1] The epigraph is from Alistair Maclean, *Hebridean Altars: The Spirit of an Island Race,* Wipf & Stock, 2013, p.9. Used by permission of Wipf and Stock Publishers wipfandstock.com.

1 Edinburgh Thoughts

[1] Ian Bradley, *The Celtic Way*, Darton, Longman & Todd, 2003 (2nd edition).
[2] Alistair Maclean, *Hebridean Altars*, p.11. Used by permission of Wipf and Stock Publishers wipfandstock.com.

2 In the Beginning . . .

[1] Peter Ryder, *Holy Columba*, 2019.
[2] E. H. B., 'Sing and they will come – How evensong is driving up attendances in Britain's cathedrals', *The*

Economist, 4 March 2014. https://www.economist .com/prospero/2014/03/04/sing-and-they-will-come.

[3] Meredee Berg, *Church of England Resurrects Tradition to Attract Millennials,* ChurchLeaders.com, 25 September 2017. https://churchleaders.com/news/ international/310736-evensong-church-of-england-resurrects-tradition-attract-millennials.html.

[4] Church Army's Research Unit, '"Not as Difficult as you Think" Mission with Young Adults', 2018. https://www .churcharmy.org/Publisher/File.aspx?ID=202434.

[5] Ray Simpson, *Exploring Celtic Spirituality*, Kevin Mayhew Ltd, 2004, p.153.

[6] Alistair Maclean, *Hebridean Altars*, p.98. Used by permission of Wipf and Stock Publishers wipfandstock.com.

3 The Right Time for the Celtic Tradition?

[1] Ian Bradley, *Celtic Christianity: Making Myths and Chasing Dreams*, Edinburgh University Press, 1999.

[2] Alexander Carmichael, *Carmina Gadelica: Hymns and Incantations*, Floris Books, 2006.

[3] David Adam, *The Holy Island of Lindisfarne*, SPCK, 2009.

[4] G. K. Chesterton, *The G.K. Chesterton Collection*, Aeterna Press, 2015.

[5] Acts of the Apostles 17:22–29.

[6] G. R. D. McLean, *Prayers of the Western Highlanders*, SPCK, 2008, p.92.

[7] Eugene Peterson, *The Message: The Bible in Contemporary Language*, Tyndale House, 2014.

[8] Brendan O'Malley, *A Celtic Primer: The Complete Celtic Worship Resource and Collection*, Hymns Ancient and Modern Ltd, 2002, p.148.

[9] Alistair Maclean, *Hebridean Altars*, p.6. Used by permission of Wipf and Stock Publishers wipfandstock .com.

4 Points of Connection: Creation and Closeness

[1] Email from the Reverend Dr Liz Hoare, to author, February 2020.

[2] Gerard Manley Hopkins, *God's Grandeur and Other Poems*, Courier Corp., 1995, p.15.

[3] Brendan O'Malley, *A Celtic Primer: The Complete Celtic Worship Resource and Collection*, Hymns Ancient and Modern Ltd, 2002, p.37.

[4] Ibid., p.93.

[5] G. R. D. McLean, *Prayers of the Western Highlanders*, SPCK, 2008, p.79.

[6] Ibid., p.29.

[7] Richard Woods, *The Spirituality of the Celtic Saints*, Orbis Books, 2000, p.153.

[8] Peter Ryder, *Holy Columba*, 2019.

[9] G. R. D. McLean, *Prayers of the Western Highlanders*, p.73.

[10] See https://www.poetryfoundation.org/poems/44477/ode-on-a-grecian-urn, accessed 27.04.20.

[11] Alexander Carmichael, *Charms of the Gaels: Hymns and Incantations*, Lindisfarne Press, 1992, p.122.

[12] Email from Dave Bookless to the author 16.2.20.

5 Points of Connection: Covering

[1] Alexander Carmichael, *Carmina Gadelica: Hymns and Incantations*, Floris Books, 2006, p.60.

[2] G. R. D. McLean, *Prayers of the Western Highlanders*, p.87.

[3] Calvin Miller, *The Path of Celtic Prayer: An ancient way to contemporary joy*, Bible Reading Fellowship, 2008, p.54.

[4] William Hughes Mulligan, *Mulligan's Law: The Wit and Wisdom of William Hughes Mulligan*, Fordham University Press, 1997, p.91.

[5] Calvin Miller, *The Path of Celtic Prayer*, p.98.

6 Points of Connection: Creativity and the Poetic Imagination

[1] Walter Brueggemann, *Hopeful Imagination: Prophetic Voices in Exile*, SCM, 1992.

[2] Ibid., p.15.

[3] E. E. Cummings, *100 Selected Poems,* 'who knows if the moon's', Grove Press, 1959.

[4] Carol Kelly-Gangi, *365 Days with the Saints: A Year of Wisdom with the Saints*, Wellfleet Press, 2015, p.96.

[5] Ray Simpson, *Exploring Celtic Spirituality*, p.157.

[6] Ian Bradley, *The Celtic Way*, Chapter 5.

[7] G. R. D. McLean, *Prayers of the Western Highlanders*, SPCK, 2008, p.25.

[8] David Adam, *Border Lands: The Best of David Adam's Celtic Vision*, Rowman & Littlefield, 1999, p.112.

[9] G. R. D. McLean, *Prayers of the Western Highlanders*, p.93.

7 Points of Connection: Communities

[1] See https://www.campaigntoendloneliness.org/loneliness-research/ (accessed 24 October 2019).

8 Justice

[1] Lilla Watson, *About Lilla Watson*. https://lillanetwork.wordpress.com/about/ (accessed 15 November 2018).

[2] See Craig Barnes, *In Search of the Lost Feminine*, Fulcrum, 2006.

9 Saints Alive

[1] Evelyn Underhill, *Evelyn Underhill's Prayer Book*, SPCK, 2018, p.19.

[2] Ibid.

[3] Esther de Waal, *The Celtic Way of Prayer: Recovering the Religious Imagination*, Canterbury Press, 2010, p.162.

[4] See David Adam, *Fire of the North: The Life of St Cuthbert*, SPCK, 2008. I am hugely indebted to the work of David Adam in this example and others.

[5] Galatians 5:6 (NIV).

10 Pilgrimage and Holy Places

[1] *The Way*, directed by Emilio Estevez, Elixir Films, 2010.

11 Our Celtic Service

[1] Matthew 11:29 (MSG).

[2] G. R. D. McLean, *Prayers of the Western Highlanders*, SPCK, 2008, p.72.

[3] Ibid., p.117.

[4] Ibid., 'Foreword'.

[5] See https://www.irishcentral.com/culture/may-the-road -rise-to-meet-you-meaning-irish-blessing (accessed 25 October 2019).

[6] Alexander Carmichael, *Carmina Gadelica: Hymns and Incantations*, Floris Books, 2006, p.257.

12 Final Word – Jesus, Our Church and the Celtic Tradition

[1] G. R. D. McLean, *Prayers of the Western Highlanders*, SPCK, 2008, p.10.

[2] Alexander Carmichael, *New Moon of the Seasons: Prayers from the Highlands and Islands*, Steiner Books, 1992, p.296.

Our Precious Lives

*Why telling and hearing
stories can save the church*

Steve Morris

Jesus was the master storyteller, powerfully relating
accessible stories to convey the good news, and Steve
Morris calls us to reclaim the art of storytelling in the
church today.

In a world of increasing social fragmentation and
loneliness, this book demonstrates how listening to others
can be transformational in creating a sense of belonging.
Inspiring stories are grounded by practical ideas to put
storytelling at the heart of the church, and questions in
each chapter encourage us all to glimpse more of God,
revel in our uniqueness and realize that we all have
something valuable to offer as his followers.

Underpinned by practical pastoral experience, this is a
book full of quirky and unexpected life stories that open
us up afresh to the beauty of life and our God.

978-1-78893-079-6

The Journey Home

*40 Days of
thoughts, prayers and
encouragement
from the Celts*

Steve Morris

Catch a glimpse of the infectious optimism of the Celtic Christians through these comforting songs, prayers, poems and devotions as we rediscover the value of community, feasting, singing and the joy of creation.

The ancient words of the Celts still sparkle with faith in a personal, ever-present God, whose care is seen in the details of creation, even when they feel endangered. Like them, in troubled times, what we long for is a sense of the nearness of God in our everyday lives.

This inspiring book encourages us to see that our true home and safety can be found in God.

978-1-78893-195-3

Front-Line Advent

*Daily thoughts, prayers
and encouragement
for Advent*

*Steve Morris
with Barry Hingston*

Advent is a time of reflection. We wonder about the great
theme of darkness and light. We think about what it is to
have faith, and to be peaceful and joyful, even when the
world seems a dangerous and unreliable place. And we
look again at the extraordinary claim that the God who
made the heavens came among us as one of us.

Based on the Lectionary readings for Year B, these daily
thoughts include reflections on beautiful poems, prayers,
explorations of Bible verses and questions to ponder.

Challenging, thought-provoking and inspirational, these
daily reflections will help us to think, pray and be aware of
God's presence in new ways this Advent.

978-1-78893-196-0

Overflow

*Learning from the
inspirational resource
church of Antioch in
the book of Acts*

Matthew Porter

The church described in Acts provides a clear biblical
example of a resource church that overflows with the
presence and power of God into their region with all the
resources God gives.

By demonstrating the characteristics, structures and
strategies that any community of Christ-followers desiring
to reach out beyond themselves can adopt, Matthew
Porter shows how we can learn to give away what God
gives and be encouraged to make steps to become a church
that overflows with the good news of Christ.

Overflow is for anyone who wants to see their church
have an overflowing impact on their surroundings and
who wants to play a part, however big or small, in seeing
churches renewed and society transformed.

978-1-78893-125-0

Mission in Marginal Places

The Stories

Paul Cloke & Mike Pears
(Eds)

The Mission in Marginal Places book series aims to provoke new understandings about how to respond to a very basic question: how might Christians respond to the Spirit's invitation to participate in God's love for the world, and especially in places of suffering and healing, of reconciliation and justice?

The third book, *The Stories*, is an exploration of the processes and practices of 'storying' mission; of listening to others and then telling appropriate stories about interconnected lives.

978-1-78078-185-3

Also available:
Mission in Marginal Places: The Praxis
978-1-84227-910-6
Mission in Marginal Places: The Theory
978-1-84227-909-0

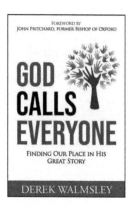

God Calls Everyone

Finding our place in his great story

Derek Walmsley

What are we supposed to do with our lives? Does God have a plan for us?

If you have ever asked these questions, then this book will help you to discern what your vocation might be. Through the lens of the Bible's whole narrative, you are invited to take part in God's story, and what he is doing, rather than asking what we can do for God. Questions at the end of each chapter allow you to reflect on the characteristics and attitudes needed for serving God.

Whether you are considering full-time ministry or wondering where you fit into God's plan, this is an accessible and engaging look at the joyous celebration of God calling us all to be part of his story.

978-1-78893-108-3

**Succession or
Multiplication?**

*Transitioning a movement to
next generation leadership*

David Devenish

How do you transition from a first generation movement
under one founder leader to becoming a second
generation movement with a multiple leadership?

This question has now become a particular challenge for
many fresh movements of churches, and it can prove to
be a difficult and daunting one. David Devenish tells the
story of how Newfrontiers tackled this issue, and how they
successfully transitioned to next generation leadership
through multiplication of leadership teams rather than
appointing a successor, while still maintaining ministry
accountability.

Combining practical lessons with academic study,
Devenish brings a wealth of experience, insight, and
guidance that will prove invaluable to other movements
embarking on a similar journey.

978-1-78893-154-0

Infused with Life

*Exploring God's gift of rest in
a world of busyness*

Andy Percey

In a stressful, task-orientated life, we know the importance of rest, but it is too often pushed out of our busy schedules.

Join Andy Percey as he reveals that rest is actually God's good gift to us, provided for us to experience a balance in our lives that isn't just about rest as recovery, but rest as harmony with our Creator and the world he has made.

By learning to practise life-giving rhythms of rest, we can be infused with the very best of the life God freely gives us.

978-1-78893-065-9